파이썬 프로그래밍

코딩영어

저자 김용찬

고려대학교에서 행정학을 전공하고, 북일리노이대학교에서 컴퓨터사이언스로 석사, 숭실대학교 경영학과 박사 과정을 수료했다. 1987년 LG-CNS 본사 연구소 팀장으로 재직하였으며 우신전자통신(주)의 SW 개발부 부장과 이사, 국내 최초의 전화정보서비스 회사인 데이텔(주)를 창업해 대표이사를 역임. 2003년부터 2009년까지 서강대학교 영상대학원 겸임교수로 재직하였고, 숭실대학교 경영학과와 노사발전재단, 숭실대학교 대학원 컴퓨터학과 등에서 강의하였다.

저서로는 『콘셉트 경영』(2018, 원펀치), 『컨셉팅하라 그리고 코딩하라』(2019, 원펀치)가 있다.

파이썬 프로그래밍 코딩영어

발행일	2022년 4월 11일
지은이	김용찬
펴낸이	김용찬
펴낸곳	원펀치
출판등록	2018. 3. 15(제2018-000018호)
주소	서울시 동작구 상도로37길 64, 501호(상도동)
홈페이지	www.ManagementByConcept.com
전화번호	010-5323-8181
이메일	palhana@naver.com

편집/디자인	(주)북랩
제작처	(주)북랩 www.book.co.kr

ISBN   979-11-963455-4-9 13000 (종이책)   979-11-963455-5-6 15000 (전자책)

파이썬 프로그래밍

코딩영어

PYTHON PROGRAMMING

CODING ENGLISH

김용찬 지음

팔하나
Palhana
8-1

'영춘권'이라고 있습니다. 제가 알기론 수많은 권법들이 있었으나 모두가 자신의 이론을 체계화시켜서 어떤 방법론을 택하는 길이었습니다. 허나 이 새로운 권법은 모든 이론을 무시하고선 오로지 승부에서 이기는 길만을 택했고, 가장 최단 시간에 상대를 제압하는 권법으로 이름을 드날리게 되었다 합니다.

코딩을 배우는 길에도 여러 이론들이 나와 있습니다. 하지만 전 오로지 가장 최단 시간에 코딩을 익혀 내는 길을 찾아냈다고 감히 선언합니다. 영어를 쓰는 사람들이 배우는 방식입니다. 영어를 모국어로 쓰지 않는 사람들이 그네들과 똑같은 방법으로 배우는 것입니다. 자기주도학습. 4~6개월이면 귀가 뻥 뚫립니다. 코딩을 영어로 바로 배운다 해서 그냥 '코딩영어'라 이름을 붙였습니다. '일언이폐지—言以蔽之'입니다.

「코딩영어」 교재가 '내 웹사이트 만들기'까지 나왔습니다. 여기까지면 후학들이 쉽게 영어로 바로 요즘 핫한 AI Deep Learning 학습엘 들어갈 수 있게 해 줍니다. 일단 책 첫 버전을 여기까지 마감해서 출판 작업에 들어가겠습니다.

CONTENTS

PART II

파이썬 중급: Blob world pygame 만들기

CONTENTS _ □ ×

PART III

Django web development: Tutorial model

PART I

파이썬 초급:
text-based tic tac toe game 만들기

처음 코딩할 때 영어 speech를 들으면서 실습하는 습관을 길들이는 것은 매우 중요합니다! 대한민국 모든 청소년들이 너도 나도 코딩영어로 무장해 담대하게 세상에 나아가게 해 드리는 것이 저희의 목표입니다. 저희가 개발한 이 자기주도학습법이 왜 우수할까요?

1. 코딩은 영어로 만든 용어요, 문법이라 영어로 들었을 때 가장 쉽게 이해가 가게 되어 있다.
2. 실습을 해서 결과가 맞게 나오면 영어가 들렸다는 얘기니깐, 혼자서도 학습이 절로 된다.
3. 정 이해가 안 되고 실습 결과가 계속 다르게 나오면, 그땐 코딩영어의 도움을 받으면 된다.

유튜브에서 강의 제목과 'sentdex'로 검색하심 Harrison Kinsley의 원본 비디오가 나옵니다. LC training(6:20). 괄호 안의 숫자는 거기 비디오가 시작되는 지점을 말합니다.

파이썬 프로그래밍 **코딩영어**

Python 프로그래밍을 하려면 다음 세 가지를 요한다 합니다:

1. understand what programming actually is
2. learn a few basic tool set - syntax, if, functions, for, while
3. use those tools, don't need big tool sets

Why Python?

1. the rapid way you can develop
2. beginner's language
3. can do anything
4. Python practice is not slow

Lookup Python tutorial usually

Go ahead and get Python - python.org - download: 64bit windows, amd64 executable installer 3.7.1 version

좀 까다로우니깐, Python download 하는 과정을 보여 줍니다:

1. check two check boxes - install launcher for all users (recommended), Add Python 3.7 to PATH
2. Install Now
3. Disable path length limit

And install an Integrated Development Environment:

1. google sublime text 3 and get there
2. grab windows 64 bit
3. install

그리곤 sublime text 3 창을 띄운 후, 파일을 하나 py3tutorial.py란 이름으로 저장한다. 이때 주의해서 file extension으로 .py이 붙는지를 살핍니다.
첫 프로그래밍으로 string을 한줄 프린트해 봅니다:

```
print("Hello Universe")
```

Anyway let's go ahead and get Python i thought i hit back but i guess i didn't So let's go to downloads and you could hit 3.7 right here so yes i'm on a windows machine A lot of people will be like ah why not Linux It just doesn't matter use whatever operating system you want to use it just does not matter So yes i'm on windows and so what i'm gonna do is i'm gonna look i'm on a 64 bit version of windows I believe the default gives you 32 bit which i wish it didn't because your with 32 bit you're limited to 2 gigabytes of RAM which is kind of silly mm-hmm Now why let's see if maybe i'll click 3 7 1 here scroll down right So i want the you know AMD 64, executable installer Obviously if you're on a 32 bit version of windows go ahead and get that one But if you have 64 bit go ahead and keep using 64 bit Also Python on windows is just traditionally one of the more difficult ones to get around certain errors so it'll be a little more useful for me to show people how to get around them So install it launcher will go ahead and also check this box to add Python to your path and then you could customize the installation but i'm just gonna go ahead and install it now and that's fun So we'll wait for that and then when we're done once you have the programming language you need something that's called like an IDE it's an integrated development environment basically Actually the I is for integrated and this is just where you write your code So this is your interpreter Sometimes or usually it kind of doubles as a place for you to write your code then also interpret the code and run it and all that you can use either the one that comes with Python which is idle just IDLE I used to use that a lot i'm a big fan of very simple editors I'm also going to disable this path length limit here i really like simple editors

2 Tuples, strings, loops

새로 tutorials라는 파일 directory를 하나 바탕화면에다 만들어 낸다. 그리곤 sublime text 3를 열어서 거기 directory에다 tutorial2.py 파일을 하나 새로 만든다. 거기서 두 번째 프로그램을 실습합니다.

variable programming_languages를 선언하고선 네 가지의 programming language 종류를 리스트 형식으로 정의해 준다. variable의 type이 궁금해서 프린트 control + b 해서 보니 tuple이라고 나온다. 더 이상은 알 필요가 없는데 그 이유? 우린 이 과정에서 그냥 just solve your problem 만을 원하기 때문! 이것 저것 기웃거리면서 아실 필요가 없어요!

다음 for loop을 실습하는 순서. 여기서 language는 temporary variable이라 합니다. for loop문 안에서만 쓰이기 때문.

여기서 sublime text 3 에다 indentation setting을 해 줘야 합니다:

1. tab width: 4
2. Convert indentation to spaces

그러곤 for loop 으로 iterate 해서 그 temporary variable에 있는 language를 하나씩 프린트해서 나오는지를 실습해 봅니다.

끝으로 'python 3.7 tuple'로 찾아서 3.7 version에서 tuples에 대한 설명이 나오는 부분을 함 찾아 봅니다.(googling 이라 함)

```python
programming_languages = "Python", "Java", "C++", "C#"
# print(type(programming_languages))
for language in programming_languages:
    print(language)
```

Imagine if you want to just dictate how you would how you would go over this You could say you know for each of these Let's you know maybe output them in some way So we know print to outputs So it's you just using natural language We would say you know for each of the languages in programming language print the language correct or something like that so So what you could say it's literally for language and so language becomes this little temporary variable here So for language in programming languages colon and then enter because we're going to start a new code block underneath this for So anytime you've got you know the definition of a function or a for loop a while loop later on we'll do some if statements stuff like that If something is the case colon new line and then you'll see that the editor just automatically tabbed it over for me Also let's talk about tabs really quick I see that it has given me a silly tab that's a mistake Let me see if i can fix that right away convert okay great So if everybody's following along and no matter what editor you're in let's make this absolutely essential change immediately So as i highlight this i can see it's just one big line that means it's a tab The problem with this is you obviously don't want to just pound your space bar four times but a tab should always be four spaces and the reason why is as you upload this maybe to github or share it with your friend who uses a different editor They might open it up and their settings might be totally different from your settings and then suddenly the tabs are the way that you sent them and then they start adding things and then suddenly they don't met mesh You've got some tabs some spaces and it just goes down very quickly So i'm just gonna left click on this I do want it to be four Google likes two but most of the world accepts four spaces So we'll keep with four and then i'm gonna say convert indentation to spaces So hopefully now you'll see dot dot dot that's what you want

3 Lists and tic tac toe game

자, 우리의 실습에 들어갑니다. text-based version of tic tac toe game을 하나 만들어 내겠습니다. 그렇담, 먼저 tic tac toe 게임이 어떻게 하는 건지를 좀 설명 드리는 것에서부터 시작해야 겠죠? 어떻게 게임이 작동하죠? 게임 룰은 뭐죠? 프로그램이 이 게임의 룰을 어떻게 알게 할 수 있을까요? 어떻게 디스플레이를 하죠? 유저로 부터 인풋 들어온 걸 어떻게 취하죠? 유저가 어디서 플레이를 한다는 걸 어떻게 알게 할까요?

어떻게 해야 할지 막연할 때엔, 좋은 솔루션이 하나 있지요. 가능한 작게 나누어서 들여다보는 겁니다. 그리곤 나중에 가서 전체를 하나로 모아 최종 product로 내놓으시는 겁니다.

첫째로 우린 게임을 위한 눈에 보이는 맵을 필요로 합니다. 맞나요?

게임 그 자체를 눈에 보이게 해 줘야 한다는 거죠. 어떻게 할까요?

GUI가 아닌 text-based니깐 우린 프로그램에서 처음 초기 값을 세팅하고선 console에서 값을 하나씩 주어 우리 게임 맵을 바꾸어 나가야 합니다. 여기서 당장 두 가지 문제에 봉착했고, 이런 식으로 해결책을 찾아냈습니다.

1. 처음엔 모두를 zero 값으로 시작하게 하고선 나중에 거기에 1이나 2등의 값을 부여해 준다. 곧, 값을 변경 가능하게 해 줘야 한다.
2. flat한 모양의 한 줄 리스트가 아닌 가로 세로가 균등하게 나뉘는 모양으로 게임 맵이 프린트되어 나와 보여 줘야 한다.

이제 3 x 3 grid 모양의 게임 맵이 나와 거기서 플레이가 가능해 보입니다.

```
game = [[0, 0, 0],
        [0, 0, 0],
        [0, 0, 0],]
for row in game:
```

```
      print(row)
----------------------------------------------------------------
[0, 0, 0]
[0, 0, 0]
[0, 0, 0]
[Finished in 346ms]
```

So the first thing and honestly this is this is these questions are this is how you approach any problem obviously tic-tac-toe is a super basic thing but it forces there's actually a lot of complex things associated with even just something as simple as tic-tac-toe So hopefully this approach to solving the problem will make sense to you and you can start to kind of think this way about any problem So when you've got a problem you what you have to do is just break it down into just the mote the smallest pieces that you can just start ticking off those small pieces until finally you've got your finished product So the first thing we want to do is i'm just going to go ahead and clear everything out here and let's just run that clear it up So with the game to play tic-tac-toe we need to play it on something we need some sort of game visual you know game map so to speak So to do that how do we want to actually visualize the game itself So we could do something like you know somehow visualize a bunch of emptiness and then you know or maybe make the grids like so obviously if you were to draw tic-tac-toe it's like two lines and two lines that's gonna be kind of hard We would spend a lot of tune with the whole ASCII stuff just getting everything to line up just right and depending on which editor someone uses or which consoles someone's using or what their font is that could get hairy really quickly So don't really think i want to do that necessarily So let's just keep it unbelievably basic So let's say let's just say we we're gonna work with zeros ones and twos So zeros will be just the game map so also just a thing to note later on when like we're gonna do things in terms of just using numbers but later if you wanted it and i totally if anybody is like man that's lame I wanted the two lines if that's you what you should do is when we're done here add the two lines to the representation because it's totally possible it's just not necessary but later you can convert everything you can convert zeros to be spaces then you can convert you know the ones and twos to actually be X's and O's and then you could convert every you know all the things in between you could use logic to create the two lines and stuff so i definitely encourage anybody who wants to to take that extra step

4 Built-in functions

저희 실습으로 들어가 보십시다. 앞에서 만든 게임 맵에다 우린 정확히 어딜 가르키는 지를 알 수 있게끔 해 줘야 하지 않을까요? 그래야, 우린 게임해서 표식을 남길 수 있고, 나중에 게임의 승패를 가릴 수 있게 될 테니까요. 맵의 위에다 그리고 옆에다 어느 column, row인지를 가릴 수 있는 숫자를 넣어 준다면 그게 가능해지지 않을까요?

'python 3 built in functions'라고 googling 해 보심 약 70개에 달하는 자체에서 기본적으로 제공해 그냥 쓸 수 있는 functions가 나옵니다. 거기서 enumerate( )라는 function을 찾아내어 그 기능을 들여다 봅니다: when you iterate over something, enumerate returns both the index value and the value of the thing you iterating over.

프로그램이 iterate 할 때에 index value, the value of the thing you iterating over를 동시에 돌려 줍니다.

여기서 우린 컴에선 index를 부를 때 0th, 1th, 2th, ... zeroth element, firstth element, secondth element로 불러준다는 것을 유의해야 합니다. 그리고 single line comment는 #, multi line comment는 ''' '''로 해 준다는 것도 기억 바랍니다.

```
game = [[0, 0, 0],
       [0, 0, 0],
       [0, 0, 0],]
print("  a b c")
for count, row in enumerate(game):
       print(count, row)
----------------------------------------------------------------
  a b c
0 [0, 0, 0]
1 [0, 0, 0]2 [0, 0, 0]
[Finished in 150ms]
```

But basically we probably want to have like numbers or letters at the top and then maybe numbers or letters on the side So one a or one one or whatever So the first thing is like what if we just wanted to like print some numbers up at the top how might we get around doing that Well one option is super simple We could just simply do like a print statement and say 0 1 2 Now it's not gonna be lined just right So let's just run it really quick ok So we probably really just need one space here Let's run it again and that appears to be pretty well aligned So if you wanted to move 0 1 2 you know for the actual row name all right so there's be a column name You could specify that column by 0 1 or 2 Now what about on the other side like how would we do it over here right because in it's in this print row that we would need the number Well there's a variety of things that we could do So one of the ways a basic programmer might do this is with a starting with like some sort of counter So you could say count equals zero and then in print you can continue to just print many things at a time So print row Well you could instead prints we could print count comma row so this will print count add a space and then print the row So for example if i just run this Now it's you know all zeros and we can see out top thing is messed up So let's add look probably two more spaces there that should do it yeah So now how can we get count to go up well all we need to do is do count and you could say count equals count plus one that's one way you could do it and so we could run that real quick and see okay 0 1 2 on that left-hand side for the each row The other option is a slightly more condensed plus equals one This does the exact same thing as count equals count plus one okay pretty cool Now this is not really the best way to do it in terms of you know being the best Python programmer you could be But it does get the job done

파이썬 프로그래밍 **코딩영어**

5 Indexes and slices

플레이어가 특정한 포지션 the exact spot에다 자신이 플레이한 내용을 남기려면 우선은 그 자리를 찾아낼 수 있어야 하고, 다음은 그 자리에 있는 값을 수정할 수 있어야 할텐데, 그걸 어떻게 프로그래밍으로 구현해 내죠?

먼저 첫번째 이슈는 구체적으로 게임 맵상 column, row 포지션의 displacement(변하는 위치)를 index로 지정해 내면 가능해집니다. 그걸 indexing 한다 합니다. 다음 두번째 이슈는 game map을 만들어 넬 때에 tuple이 아닌 list type으로 만들어 내면 immutable issue에서 자유로워 집니다.

이런 식으로 문제의 정의(즉, 요구사항)가 나오고, 그걸 해결해 줄 수 있는 솔루션을 찾는 것이 프로그래밍의 알파요 오메가라 할 것입니다.

이번 강좌에선 displacement, indexing에 관한 실습을 다양한 케이스로 나누어서 들여다 보겠습니다. 그 요령을 한 마디로 정리하면, indexing은 좌에서 우로 0th, 1st-th, 2nd-th, ... 우에서 좌로는 negative 1st, negative 2nd, ... 로 셈합니다. slicing 할 때엔, all the way up to the 3rd, everything after the 2nd-th 등으로 셈합니다.

```python
l = [1,2,3,4,5]
print(l[1:3])
print(l[2:])

game = [[0, 0, 0],
        [0, 0, 0],
        [0, 0, 0],]
print("   a  b  c")
game[0][1] = 1
for count, row in enumerate(game):
        print(count, row)
--------------------------------------------------------------
```

```
[2, 3]
[3, 4, 5]
   a b c
0 [0, 1, 0]
1 [0, 0, 0]
2 [0, 0, 0]
[Finished in 138ms]
```

The next thing that we want to do is like let's say a player says they want to play at a certain position How do we modify that specific position in our actual game So what we can use first of all you can use indexes to get an exact value but you can also set a value at a specific index or you could use a slice So to exemplify this what i'm gonna do is multi-line comment out what we've done so far so quote quote quote close it off here and then i'm just gonna work right above here and just make some space So let's say we've got a list i'm gonna say I equals and we're just going to say 1 2 3 4 5 just for quick reference to reference an index of a list We can say I and then in square brackets we put the index So let's say I 1 so the thing that's at the first-th index what should that be Well it's going to be the 2 right because the 1 is the 0-th index So if we were to print this out we can see ok we get a 2 here Now the other thing that we can do is we can do more fancy things like for example we can even do like so what if we wanted to reference that 5 Well the 5 would be at index 4 right But 5 is also at the end of the list So we could reference it with a negative 1 So at the negative 1-th element of the list also a 5 We can also reference a slice So we can reference from the first th to the third index and you can see here it is a 2 to a 3 So the 1th is this 2 all the way up to the 3rd which is the 3 We could go like this or if you wanted to do everything from a certain point you could say to colon form everything after the 2nd-th index and so on There's lots of stuff that we can do there

6 Functions

코딩을 하다 보면, 우린 조금씩 다르더라도 일정한 코드 블럭을 반복해서 써야 하는 경우를 자주 만나게 됩니다. 흔히들 copy & paste 해서들 쓰죠. 그러다 나중 가서 거기 어떤 variable을 수정하게 되면, 나머지 코드 블럭에서도 역시 수정해 주어야 하지만, multi lines인 경우 실수로 그걸 놓치는 경우가 발생하게 마련이지요. 결국에 가선 프로그램에 해를 끼치는 결과를 가져오는 경우가 허다합니다. 이럴 경우를 대비해서 우린 무슨 조치를 취해 줘야 하지 않을까요?

반복되는(repetitive) 코드를 우린 어떤 식으로든 편리하게 쓸 수 있는 길을 모색해 왔고, 그렇게 해서 나온 것이 function이란 기법입니다. 한번 define 해 놓고선 필요로 할 때에 불러 쓸 수 있게 해 줍니다. 그럼, 동일한 코드 묶음이 계속 반복되어 수행됩니다.

PEP8이라고 Python styling rules가 있어, variables는 lower cased, functions는 lower cased(and separated by underscore), class objects는 title cased로 쓰는 것을 따르게 하고 있습니다.

흔히들 하는 실수가 parenthesis 없이 function을 부릅니다. 그리곤 왜 아무런 일이 일어나지 않지? 합니다. 그건 parenthesis 없이 function을 부르면, 그냥 그 function을 포인트만 할 뿐 ask to run을 하는건 아니기 때문에 아무런 일이 일어나지 않는 겁니다.

어때요, 파이썬 참 쉽지 않아요?

```python
game = [[0, 0, 0],
        [0, 0, 0],
        [0, 0, 0],]
def game_board():
    print("  0 1 2")
    for count, row in enumerate(game):
        print(count, row)
game_board()
game[0][1] = 1
```

파이썬 프로그래밍 **코딩영어**

```
game_board()                                                              25
-------------------------------------------------------------------------
   0 1 2
0 [0, 0, 0]
1 [0, 0, 0]
2 [0, 0, 0]
   0 1 2
0 [0, 1, 0]
1 [0, 0, 0]
2 [0, 0, 0]
[Finished in 238ms]
```

Anyway we've got repetition of code here and what if like for example that one of the reasons aside from taking up space it's okay to get over that One other besides from taking up space the problem is later what if rather than a b c you want to call this zero one two right Then if you wanted to make that change you're gonna have to go from here and like start copying and pasting or maybe you'll get fancy and use a find and replace But what if it's like multi lines and then what if there's like slight variable changes Guess what you're gonna make a mistake and you're gonna ruin something So instead what you wanted to use and begin to use is functions So anytime you've got repetition in your code even if it's not identical like sometimes that repetition might have slight differences chances are you should be using a function or maybe even a full loop or something like that But in this case, we should definitely be using a function because we just want to like call this block of code to run pretty much every time a player has made a move So for example what if we just let's just define a function So to define a function you'll just use def space and then the function name and up to this point i really haven't talked at all about styling and like PEP 8 which is the Pythons version of all the styling rules But in general variables should all be kind of like lowercased you don't want to like camel case or title case variables like you might in other languages Functions same thing it should all be lower cased words would be separated by underscore So for the most part i do my best to keep this tutorial PEP 8 So for example so we could call this game board right That would be that's clearly so like if someone was to import your script and import game board from your script immediately people know okay that's a function as apposed to later down the line maybe you've got a class something that makes object You wouldn't call it this way You would call it in title casing which is what we use for classes and again if someone was to import that and all they saw was the name they would know immediately that's a class

7 Function parameters

repetitive code block을 우린 function으로 만들어 내고선 불러 쓴다 했다. 그때 우린 어떤 valuables를 parenthesis 안에다 parameters로 넣어 주어 define 하게 되면, function을 불러 쓸 때에 그 parameters를 활용해 add logic, manipulate variables 등 원하는 일들을 수행하게 할 수 있게 된다.

파이썬에선 variables를 선언할 때 data type을 미리 지정하지 않는다. 실제 불러 쓸 때에 그 data 값으로 무엇을 주느냐에 따라 data type이 자동으로 정해지는데 이 기능을 일컬어 dynamically typed, dynamic typing이라 한다.

```python
game = [[0, 0, 0],
    [0, 0, 0],
    [0, 0, 0],]

def game_board(player=0, row=0, column=0, just_display=False):
    print("  0 1 2")
    if not just_display:
        game[row][column] = player # put a value on the
    entry
    for count, row in enumerate(game):
        print(count, row)       # just print the board

game_board(just_display=True)
game_board(player=1, row=0, column=1)
--------------------------------------------------------------------
  0 1 2
0 [0, 0, 0]
1 [0, 0, 0]
```

```
2 [0, 0, 0]
0 [0, 1, 0]
1 [0, 0, 0]
2 [0, 0, 0]
[Finished in 346ms]
```

The only other thing i might say here is maybe if we said like we definitely want to have some sort of handling for how you know how do we want to actually display the game if we didn't pass anything here so And the other thing to note is like let's see so what we could say here is just if player not actually does not equal zero or something like that whoops and then just tab this over then play it this way You also could have like a little flag like that might even make more sense like just display and just display could equal false to start and then instead you could say if not just display it was false so then you could say here just display equals true In this case if we scroll up we get just the purely display and we didn't set 0 0 equals 0 because again if let's say someone had actually played at that 0, 0 mark we would be in trouble alright So now if just display is equal to true so if not just display so if just display we're not gonna actually run this code and then Otherwise no matter what happens we want to print out the game board

8 Mutability revisited

function에서 바꾼 variables의 값이 function 바깥으로 나왔을 때에도 여전히 변한 상태로 유지되어 있을까? 그걸 몇 차례 실험을 통해서 살펴보았더니, 언제나 그렇지는 못했다. 실제로는 몇 몇 경우 variables 값이 바뀌지 않았던 것이다. 그렇담, 우린 우리의 코드에서 신뢰를 갖지 못하게 될 것이다. 과연 무슨 조치를 취하면 우리의 코드가 consistent 하게 신뢰를 갖추게 할 수 있을까? 이번 이슈를 list, tuple의 mutable, immutable issue round-1에 이어 mutable, immutable issue round-2 라 합니다. 결론은 function이 끝날 때 그 value 값을 return 하게 되면, 언제나 mutable data값을 갖게 할 수 있습니다.

```
quiz:
x=1          # tuple is immutable, 노!
def test():
      x=2
test()
print(x)


x=1          # global은 언제든 예스!
def test():
      global x
      x=2
test()
print(x)


x=[1,2,3]    # list라서 바꾸는 게 예스!
def test():
      x[1]=0
test()
```

```python
print(x)

x=[1]                # list의 값은 index를 이용해 바꾸어야 해요, 노!
def test():
        x=[2]
test()
print(x)


x=[1]                # global은 언제든 예스!
def test():
     global x
     x=[2]
test()
print(x)


x=[1]                # index를 썼으니 list에서 작동, 예스!
def test():
     x[0]=2
test()
print(x)
```

실습:
```python
game = [[0, 0, 0],
      [0, 0, 0],
      [0, 0, 0],]

def game_board(game_map, player=0, row=0, column=0,
just_display=False):
     if not just_display:
          game_map[row][column] = player
     for count, row in enumerate(game_map):
          print(count, row)
     return game_map

game = game_board(game, just_display=True)
game = game_board(game, player=1, row=2, column=-1)
----------------------------------------------------------------
0 [0, 0, 0]
1 [0, 0, 0]
```

```
2 [0, 0, 0]
0 [0, 0, 0]
1 [0, 0, 0]
2 [0, 0, 1]
[Finished in 143ms]
```

I also have passed in the text-based version of this tutorial I put in a little quiz and Daniel or Danos from the discord wrote up I think it's actually a pretty good quiz on So if you want i'll have the link to the text-based version of this tutorial in the description Go there and like copy and paste this code into like some script or something And beside all the X's are on a sheet of paper or whatever say okay here's what i think X is going to be equal to right And then run it and see how you did Even after like seven years of Python i still missed one of them It was uh i don't really want to talk about it necessarily But it was this one here and at least i think it was the i want to say was the middle one yeah okay It was that one and you know maybe for you guys or people that are following along that have nothing to do with basics maybe you miss nothing on this test But my argument is if you missed anything on this little quiz or you had to think kind of hard about it chances are when you're like zooming through writing a program that's how i program by the way You are highly likely to make the mistake So the whole point of this tutorial has been one to draw your attention to how you can run yourself amok with mutability but also i would argue we should go ahead and just pass game here or maybe better put let's call it game map or apparently game board where did that come from oh that's name of the function Let's not do that so we'll call it game map So we pass game map i would argue let's go ahead and call this game map So we're going to modify this temporary game map variable here game map game map enumerate game map And then when we're all done return game map

9 Error handling

우린 코드를 짜다 보면 아래와 같이 언제 어디서 어떤 에러가 날지 대충 짐작을 할 수 있습니다:

1. user 입장에선 variable index가 어디까지인지를 순간적으로 잊어버립니다.
2. 프로그래머 입장에선 variable name, function name을 실수나 혼동해서 타이핑합니다.

이런 경우를 대비해, 거기에다 try, except 문으로 code block을 나눠줘서 각기 적합한 메시지를 낼 수 있게끔 에러처리를 해 놓으면, 나중에 에러가 발생하더라도 당장 프로그램 수행이 중단되지 않습니다. 그리고 그 에러에 대한 컨트롤이 쉽게 가능해진답니다.

또 윈도우에선 간단히 파일탐색기 file path directory(address bar) 상에서 cmd 를 치는 것으로 console(command) mode로 들어갈 수 있다는 걸 알게 되었습니다.

```python
game = [[0, 0, 0],
     [0, 0, 0],
     [0, 0, 0],]

def game_board(game_map, player=0, row=0, column=0,
just_display=False):
    try:
        if not just_display:
            game_map[row][column] = player
        for count, row in enumerate(game_map):
            print(count, row)
        return game_map
    except IndexError as e:
```

```
            print("Error: make sure you input row/column as 0,
    1, or 2?", e)
        except Exception as e:
            print("Something went very wrong!", e)


game = game_board(game, just_display=True)
game = game_board(game_board, player=1, row=3, column=-1)
------------------------------------------------------------
0 [0, 0, 0]
1 [0, 0, 0]
2 [0, 0, 0]
Something went very wrong! 'function' object is not
subscriptable
[Finished in 134ms]
```

Maybe now would be a good moment for us to address running things from the console The other way you would actually run a program is probably not in your editors So let's go ahead and open up a console so on you know at least on Linux you can right click an open console here or open terminal here on Windows you can just come to the address bar up there and just type cmd and that'll open up a terminal right where we are and ctrl + is not a valid Let's see properties and see if i can do this quickly let's go 28 ok good enough So now let's say we want to run tutorial 9 So the way we would do that is one you could type just Python and currently that is referencing Python 3.7 for me But if you have multiple versions of Python by the way quit() is a built-in function and you can exit that's just typed by default Now i just type it you could also do like you price you should be able to get away with can maybe control you can't get out with control C so anyways What do we do if we want to actually run a Python program We'll if you want to specify you could say py - 3.7 if i hit enter here it still opens up the same version i'm on So we could say Python 3.7 and then what do we want to run So i think it was tutorial run tutorial 9 So we'll run tutorial 9 and we'll actually see the very you know this is the full trace back It doesn't have that extra stuff that we saw in sublime text But basically this is the error and then it gives us a little snippet of code that it saw tells us in what file did we see it in most cases when you get an error like this The real error that you're looking for is at the bottom of your script If you're working in a much larger project though sometimes it can get buried because the trace back literally a trace is back the error and goes in the order that the program ran So sometimes at the end of your code or at the end of the trace back it does have an error but the thing that caused that error is sometimes buried deep because it was a different script that errored and then the errors transgress okay continue through until we got to your the current place that you're working So sometimes it won't be at the very bottom but this is always what you're looking for

10 Calculating horizontal winner

드디어 game winner를 찾아내는 알고리즘(연산, procedure) 차례입니다.

우린 게임보드상에서 어떤 상황일 때 winner가 나오고 게임이 중단되어야 하는지를 살필 수 있어 야 겠습니다. 세 가지 경우가 예상되는데, 그 첫번째가 어느 한 player가 수평적으로 모든 땅을 다 점했을 때이며, 이를 horizontal winner라 부릅니다. 동일한 row 내에서 각기 다른 column이 row[0] == row[1] == row[2] 인 경우이며, 이는 간략히 row.count(row[0]) == len(row) 로 코딩해 서 체크가 가능하다는 것을 googling 'check if all elements in a list are identical' 해서 나온 stack overflow 예문에서 찾았고, 응용했습니다.

```python
game = [[1, 1, 1],
        [0, 2, 0],
        [2, 2, 0],]
'''
def win(current_game):
    for row in game:
        print(row)
        col1 = row[0]
        col2 = row[1]
        col3 = row[2]
        if col1 == col2 == col3:
            print("Winner!")
'''
'''
def win(current_game):
    for row in game:
        print(row)
        all_match = True
        for item in row:
```

```
                    if item != row[0]:
                        all_match = False
            if all_match:
                print("winner!!!")
'''
def win(current_game):
    for row in game:
        if row.count(row[0]) == len(row) and row[0] !=0:
            print("Winner!")
win(game)
----------------------------------------------------------------
Winner!
[Finished in 245ms]
```

We can do it this way but what happens when your boss comes to you and says hey Johnny we really like what you do with the 3 x 3 tic-tac-toe Make it a 4 x 4 now and then you're like dang it! and then you're like okay but that's okay I will just go into my code and changes in super simple right But then what happens when your boss comes back and don't forget you've done this now for however you decided to calculate vertical and diagonal Then your boss comes back and they're like hey Johnny um can we make the game size of tic tac toe dynamic? And at this point you are going to have a pretty big problem because you've hard-coded this so then you might be thinking well i can't do dynamic but what i can do is i could have a separate tic-tac-toe like i have a 3 x 3 version i could have 4 x 4 and 5 x 5 and all that like i could just have a separate script and that's not good that's what i would describe as disgusting okay But through my career of doing contracting consulting for various companies i've seen people do that i've seen people have a thousand or more variations of a script that is otherwise identical except for like one variable change Don't do that That's called technical debt and you do not want it like the first time you program something like that okay i guess maybe you'll get away with it But then over time as things change where you need to make minor changes suddenly you need to write a Python program to make the changes So this isn't ideal So we know because we've talked about repetition and stuff we know this is probably not right Then we are thinking okay we'll what if we do that initial idea where it's like you know we iterate over the rows and then maybe not match flag could be like false

⑪ Vertical winners

동일한 column에서 모두 같은 player가 땅을 따먹었다면, 그건 vertical winner가 됩니다. 알고리즘 구현을 위해 check = [ ], columns = [0, 1, 2]를 활용했다가, console mode에서 range( ) built-in function 기능을 확인해 보고선, range(len(game)) 을 활용합니다.

```python
game = [[2, 0, 1],
        [0, 0, 1],
        [2, 2, 1],]


columns = [0, 1, 2]
for col in columns:
        check = []
        for row in game:
                check.append(row[col])
                print(check)
                if check.count(check[0]) == len(check) and
                check[0] !=0:
                print("Winner!")
```

여기서 우린 console mode로 가서 python -3.7(multiple version인 경우) 혹은 python 으로 들어가 range function(an immutable sequence type)을 실습해 기능을 확인합니다:

```
C:\Windows\System32>python
Python 3.7.2 (tags/v3.7.2:9a3ffc0492, Dec 23 2018, 23:09:28) [MSC
v.1916 64 bit (AMD64)] on win32
Type "help", "copyright", "credits" or "license" for more
information.
```

```
>>> x = range(3)
>>> for i in x:
...         print(i)
...
0
1
2
>>>
```

최종 버전. 이 range( )를 적용했더니 매우 간결하게 coding이 되어 나왔습니다.

```
for col in range(len(game)):
        check = []
        for row in game:
                check.append(row[col])
                print(check)
        if check.count(check[0]) == len(check) and check[0] !=0:
                print("Winner!")
----------------------------------------------------------------------
[2]
[2, 0]
[2, 0, 2]
[0]
[0, 0]
[0, 0, 2]
[1]
[1, 1]
[1, 1, 1]
Winner!
[Finished in 136ms]
```

But columns basically we could just say columns is like if you just wanted to iterate 0 1 2 what probably the best way is with a range So again range is not something that we've talked about but it's a built-in function in Python so let me do built-in Python functions really? built-in Python functions 3.7 maybe i'm surprised that wasn't like the top result I must have typed it different than normal Anyway we can come down to range and we can actually see that range Is it going to explain range? Anyway okay yeah it does rather than being a function range is actually an immutable sequence type So it's actually not a function but we treat it like a function So it's okay we all just we it's included in the built-in functions because we treat it like one but in the backend is actually not a function it's a much it's much more efficient and the reason why you'd want that is in theory you could do you know range of like a huge number and that won't blow your memory But if you were to do something to convert it to a list for example and make that a list of that size that will absolutely blow your memory So let me open up the command window real quick and let's run py dash 3 point not three six three seven i'm so used to typing three six there okay And let's just say an X equals range three and then like for i in x print i you get zero one two okay So it just iterates over that and it's not quite a list it's al it's much more efficient than a list and we'll see later that there's other operations that we can do on this that are similar operations to what we could do to a list as well so anyways that's how i thing we should go about it We're basically this number three is just the len of the game

⑫ Diagonal winners

win(game)의 마지막 순서로 diagonal winner를 찾아내는 알고리즘 입니다. 두 경우를 예상할 수 있는데, \ / 입니다.

```python
if game[0][0] == game[1][1] == game[2][2]:
    print("Winner")
if game[2][0] == game[1][1] == game[0][2]:
    print("Winner")
```

이걸 dynamic하게 코딩해 내려면 다음과 같이 해야 할 겁니다.

```python
diags = []
for ix in range(len(game)):
    diags.append(game[ix][ix])

diags = []
cols = list(reversed(range(len(game))))
rows = range(len(game))
for idx in rows:
    print(idx, cols[idx])
```

다만, 여기서 아랫 / 로직은 이렇게 좀은 더 쉽게 코딩을 해낼 수가 있겠습니다.

```
diags = []
cols = reversed(range(len(game)))
rows = range(len(game))
for col, row, in zip(cols, rows):
      print(col, row)
```

다시 더 명료하게

```
for col, row in enumerate(reversed(range(len(game)))):
      print(col, row)

      diags.append(game[row][col])
-----------------------------------------------------------
0 2
1 1
2 0
0 2
1 1
2 0
0 2
1 1
2 0
[Finished in 143ms]
```

여기서도 우린 console mode/window로 가서 zip( ) built-in function 기능을 실험해 보는 시간을 가졌습니다. 바로 궁금한 결과를 볼 수 있으니 참 편리한 기능이라 할 것입니다.

```
C:\Windows\System32>py
Python 3.8.5 (default, Sep 3 2020, 21:29:08) [MSC v.1916 64 bit
(AMD64)] :: Anaconda, Inc. on win32
Type "help", "copyright", "credits" or "license" for more
information.
>>> x = range(3)
>>> for i in x:
...         print(i)
...
0
1
2
>>> y = [2, 1, 0]
>>> zip (x, y)

<zip object at 0x0000021506A39380>
>>> for i in zip(x, y):
...         print(i)
...
(0, 2)
(1, 1)
(2, 0)
>>> z = [5, 6, 7]
>>> a = zip(x, y, z)

>>> for i in a:
...         print(i)
...
(0, 2, 5)
(1, 1, 6)
(2, 0, 7)
>>>
```

The other thing we could say we could use enumerate for example and do kind of this very similar task that we're doing But in this case we're actually we're not trying to we're not trying to enumerate We're not just trying because like in this case we're just conveniently using idx because it happens to be actually an index right And so conveniently we are able to use it but that's not actually what we're thinking we're trying to do We are trying to combine these two things and then iterate over them and that's actually a really common task in programming And as you might suspect there's a built-in function for it It is called zip So what this is gonna do is it's just gonna aggregate elements from each notice that each of the iterables So you could continue passing multiple iterables So let's let me just quickly y equals range i don't want to do that Let's just say two one zero zip x y okay So that just creates a zip object so how about for i in zip x y print i okay You can see they've been zipped together What if we did z equals five six seven and then we just do a equals zip x y z for i in a i think i did one too many spaces there print a for i in a I'm actually kind of surprised why did it say zip object there i thought we would get away with that For i in zip x y z print i There we go

13 Bringing things together

경기를 하는 사람이 둘이라 했을 때, player 1, 2가 번갈아 가면서 경기할 기회를 주는 것이 공평하다. 문제는 이걸 코딩으로 어떻게 기회를 주게 할 수 있느냐다. 구글링 'python flip between numbers' 해서 찾아낸 것이 itertools.cycle( ) 이란 메스더다. 그리고 built-in next( ) function도 있었다. 번갈아 가면서 차례로 경기를 할 수 있게 해 주는 매직이다. 여기서 우린 iterable, iterator의 구분을 해 줄 필요가 나왔다. 전자는 a thing we can iterate over 이고, 후자는 a special object with next( ) method 즉 next( ) function을 쓸 수 있게 해 주는 게 iterator 라는 거다. iterator는 동시에 iterable 기능도 겸하고 있다는 것을 확인해 보았다. 더해서 iter( ) iterator는 reach stop iteration 기능도 한다는 것이 마냥 계속해서 반복되기만 하는 cycle iterable 기능과 대비되어 보인다.

```python
import itertools
game = [[1, 0, 2],
       [1, 1, 1],
       [1, 2, 1],]
def win(current_game):
    # Horizontal
    for row in game:
        print(row)
        if row.count(row[0]) == len(row) and row[0] !=0:
            print(f"player {row[0]} is the winner
        horizontally (-)!")


    # Diagonal
    diags = []
    for col, row in enumerate(reversed(range(len(game)))):
        diags.append(game[row][col])
```

```python
        if diags.count(diags[0]) == len(diags) and diags[0] !=0:
            print(f"player {diags[0]} is the winner diagonally
(/)!")
        diags = []
        for ix in range(len(game)):
            diags.append(game[ix][ix])
        if diags.count(diags[0]) == len(diags) and diags[0] !=0:
            print(f"player {diags[0]} is the winner diagonally
(\\)")


        # Vertical
        for col in range(len(game)):
            check = []
            for row in game:
                check.append(row[col])
            if check.count(check[0]) == len(check) and
        check[0] !=0:
                print(f"player {check[0]} is the winner vertically
(¦)")

def game_board(game_map, player=0, row=0, column=0,
just_display=False):
        try:
            if not just_display:
                game_map[row][column] = player
            for count, row in enumerate(game_map):
                print(count, row)
            return game_map
except IndexError as e:
    print("Error: make sure you input row/column as 0, 1, or
2?", e)
except Exception as e:
    print("Something went very wrong!", e)


play = True
players = [1, 2]
while play:
        game = [[0, 0, 0],
            [0, 0, 0],
```

```
        [0, 0, 0]]

game_won = False
game = game_board(game, just_display=True)
player_choice = itertools.cycle([1, 2])
while not game_won:
      current_player = next(player_choice)
      print(f"current_player: {current_player}")
      column_choice = int(input("What column do you
want to play? (0, 1, 2): "))
      row_choice = int(input("What row do you want to
play? (0, 1, 2): "))
      game = game_board(game, current_player,
row_choice, column_choice)
```

Python flip between numbers We'll see if this will come up with the same one scroll down okay yeah so this is the one i had found and i actually never heard of itertools dot cycle because as i was writing my method of doing it the way i was doing it was so ugly that i was like surely there's a way and then also i was like surely there's a way to like actually like rotate so we've seen i think it was a the cue i forget which one it was that we found before that actually has a way to rotate and then you could always use like the index of zero or something like that But so coming on let's see So let's try using itertools cycle so i so looking down here you can import cycle This is just a range of two So that would calling dot next on Now with my experience i know that's not gonna work anymore but let's try let's try how to how we would actually like do that So the other option we would have is import itertools and then we could say player choice equals itertools dot cycle and then we're gonna cycle between player 1 and 2 because we can and then for i in range of let's say 10 what could we do well we could just print player choice dot next Now i already know this is not gonna be happy but let's say you get this error right and don't forget like this stuff is sublime really If we ran this in a console we would see this So i understand what this means but you might not So again you copy that error come over here paste it in Go to this first option who cares what they're doing Let's just look at this guys what he has to say ok dot next was removed in Python 3 use next iter instead right So then he says all you have to do is take dot next and then convert it to next as the built-in function that it is So let's do that So let's just say we get rid of dot next and then we print instead next player choice boom okay so that works

파이썬 프로그래밍 **코딩영어**

14 Wrapping up tic tac toe

오늘까지 해서 text-based tic tac toe game을 하나 거뜬히 만들어 냈습니다.

13강에서 만든 알고리즘이 뭔가 잘못이 있다는 것이 밝혀졌습니다. 'bool' object is not sub-scriptable이란 에러 메시지를 얻었습니다. 다시 로직을 살펴보니 game_board를 선언할 때 우린 game_map만 value return 했지, 거기서 boolean 값은 처리해 주지 않았습니다. 그리고 main control에서 세 번의 while 문을 돌리면서 각기 세 가지 다른 boolean 값을 사용했습니다. 문제는 여기서 앞의 game_board( ) 문을 부르고 value return을 할 때 boolean 값을 game과 함께 return 해 주지 않아서 자리를 못찾은 boolean 값 때문에 에러가 났다는 사실이 밝혀진 것입니다. 고치고 나니 이젠 알고리즘이 완벽하게 돌아가는 것을 확인할 수 있었습니다.

그 외에도 join( )과 두 번의 list comprehension 문으로 game map을 dynamic 하게 구현하고 불러 쓸 수 있게 coding을 해내었습니다:

```python
game_size = int(input("what size game of tic tac toe? "))
game = [[0 for i in range(game_size)] for i in range(game_size)]

import itertools
def win(current_game): # win is True or False, it tells
    def all_same(l):
        if l.count(l[0]) == len(l) and l[0] != 0:
            return True
        else:
            return False
    # Horizontal
    for row in game:
        print(row)
        if all_same(row):
            print(f"player {row[0]} is the winner
        horizontally!")
```

```python
                return True
        # Diagonal
        diags = []
        for col, row in enumerate(reversed(range(len(game)))):
                diags.append(game[row][col])
        if all_same(diags):
                print(f"player {diags[0]} is the winner diagonally
        (/)!")
                return True
        diags = []
        for ix in range(len(game)):
                diags.append(game[ix][ix])
        if all_same(diags):
                print(f"player {diags[0]} is the winner diagonally
        (₩₩)!")
                return True
        # Vertical
        for col in range(len(game)):
                check = []
                for row in game:
                        check.append(row[col])
                if all_same(check):
                        print(f"player {check[0]} is the winner
                vertically (¦)!")
                        return True
        return False        # nobody has won
def game_board(game_map, player=0, row=0, column=0,
just_display=False):
        try:
                if game_map[row][column] != 0:
                        print("This position is occupado! Choose
                another!")
                        return game_map, False
                print(" "+" ".join([str(i) for i in
        range(len(game_map))]))
                if not just_display:
                        game_map[row][column] = player
                for count, row in enumerate(game_map):
                        print(count, row)
                return game_map, True
        except IndexError as e:
```

```python
            print("Error: make sure you input row/column as 0,
    1, or 2?", e)
            return game_map, False
        except Exception as e:
            print("Something went very wrong!", e)
            return game_map, False
play = True
players = [1, 2]
while play:
    game_size = int(input("what size game of tic tac toe? "))
    game = [[0 for i in range(game_size)] for i in
range(game_size)]
    game_won = False
    game, _ = game_board(game, just_display=True)  # _ :
nothing has returned
    player_choice = itertools.cycle([1, 2])
    while not game_won:
        current_player = next(player_choice)
        print(f"current_player: {current_player}")
        played = False
        while not played:
            column_choice = int(input("What column do
you want to play? (0, 1, 2): "))
            row_choice = int(input("What row do you want
to play? (0, 1, 2): "))
            game, played = game_board(game, current_player,
            row_choice, column_choice)
            if win(game):
                game_won = True
                again = input("The game is over, would you
            like to play again? (y/n) ")
                if again.lower() == "y":
                    print("restarting")
                elif again.lower() == "n":
                    print("Byeeeee")
                    play = False
                else:
                    print("Not a valid answer, so... c u
                later")
                    play = False
```

You know i guess part of the issue here like if this did return false later if you tried to input See we are probably getting in trouble really quickly actually Because if that returns false the game map has been redefined and we can't really let that happen now, can we? So why don't we will have to change this ever so slightly to be a return game we need to return game may and the boolean statement So let me just will do this so game map false and then here will return true and then here game map false game map false that way Now we come down here and when we play the game game we'll also get a return now in this case we don't care about the return So in Python if you don't care about one of the things that's going to be returned you use an underscore and the underscore just means it doesn't matter basically But then down here game and then played equals the following So now i guess i could just do this and now let's save that Let's rerun that and see how we did So and i think and that's why it says bool is it's not scriptable I think what was happening is it you know returns false We try to play another location and we're attempting to choose an index in a boolean which obviously it doesn't exit So 1 1 ok current player 2 1 1 we can't do that spot how about 0 1 okay so now player 2 can play at position 0 1 okay i think that works

(15) Conclusion

이 15강에선 파이썬 패키지를 사용하기 위해선 python install package 즉, pip install package 해서 쓴다는 것과, 코딩에서 그걸 import library 해서 갖다 쓴다는 것을 간단한 예제를 통해서 보여 줍니다. pip install package 할 때엔 주위에서 malicious 한 모듈들로 숱한 폐해를 입는 경우가 많으니, PyPI, Python package index 에서 standard library name을 확인한 연후에 안전한지를 가려서 pip install 하는 습관을 가져야 합니다.

tic tac toe game의 마지막 처리를 game board 상에 player를 컬러로 표시케 해 보겠습니다. 먼저 pip install colorama 하시고선, colorama - PyPI로 가서 거기서 제공하는 용법 document를 참고하시기 바랍니다. 그리곤 약간의 코드 수정으로 초급 과정 실습을 마칩니다.

파이썬 초급 과정이 끝났습니다. 어때요, 재밌지 않아요? 이제 여러분이 맛본 내용으로 자신이 재밌어하는 분야로 자유롭게 진출해 프로젝트를 해 보시기 바랍니다.

```
가 볼 만한 곳 -
>>>import antigravity
github, reddit/r/python, reddit/r/learnpython
discord.gg/sentdex
>>>import this
the zen of python, by Tim Peters, those stuffs to keep in mind
when coding
```

```python
from colorama import Fore, Back, Style, init
init()
...
for count, row in enumerate(game_map):
    colored_row = ""

    for item in row:
        if item == 0:
            colored_row += " "
        elif item == 1:
            colored_row += Fore.GREEN + ' x ' +
        Style.RESET_ALL
        elif item == 2:
            colored_row += Fore.MAGENTA + ' o ' +
        Style.RESET_ALL
    print(count, colored_row)
```

Now when you get a new package let's just google colorama There's a variety of ways that packages will document themselves and everyone no one's documentation is as good as everybody else's So you just kind of like or everyone's documentation is a little different so some packages have unbelievably great documentation it's really easy to use other packages don't and then in terms of you know complexity they all vary Colorama is pretty simple library So their documentation is basically right here on this page But certain things like Django like will have either their own website of there's a website called read the docs and that's pretty popular documentation website and so it just kind of depends But usually you can just go through the documentation and learn how to use the packages So for example i scroll on down here and i basically just scroll like here's the main thing i just scroll until i see some text that is code So in this case i can see okay so to use Colorama okay i need to initialize it alright Looks like on windows we need to run in it on the other platform It doesn't matter so this is just for cross-platform okay Now to get it to print colors all i have to do is apparently you do this then you add to the string So this is probably it's building the string so using the plus here So this fore dot red probably corresponds to a bit of code that probably looks really complex to you So for example this ANSI sequence here like this is probably more so What if actually looks like what this will translate to But this is you know a little more easy for us to type so It looks like we could change the foreground the background style and then we can reset everything And one thing to note is like when you change colors you you have to change them back So when you say fore red that means everything that comes after that is gonna have a red foreground so pay attention

난 코딩을 영어로 바로 배운다

- AI, Metaverse시대 비즈니스 환경에서 살아남기 위해 반드시 배워야 하는 영어와 코딩!
- 컴퓨터와 소통해내는 프로그래밍 언어는 유형화 有形化가 잘 되어있어서 영어를 학습하기에 적합합니다.
- LC w/ Py - 파이썬 프로그래밍으로 배우는 영어 Listening Comprehension 학습프로그램이 탄생한 이유
- 코딩학습은 약간의 필수 문법만 익히고선 곧장 재밌는 프로젝트로 달려갈 수 있게 해주는 방식이 최선
- 마침 Sentdex사에서 제공하는 1,000개가 넘는 주옥과 같은 파이썬 동영상 학습 프로그램이 유튜브에 올라 있습니다. 지금도 꾸준히 숙달된 강사를 통해서 파이썬 강좌를 열어가고 있습니다. 우리가 영어를 배우기엔 딱~^인 학습교재!
- NIU에서 컴사이를 전공한 선후배, 김용찬과 윤비아 둘이서 이 콘텐츠를 개발. 중학생 이상이면 누구든 쉽게 자기주도로 학습할 수 있게, LC훈련을 통해 영어 비디오를 요점정리.
- 귀가 뚫리면서 영어에 자신을 갖게 해드립니다. 동시에 파이썬을 자연스럽게 익히는 부수효과도 가져다 줌

영어, 파이썬을 귀하의 경쟁력으로

월수 19:30-21:30 서울 마포구 신촌로 102-1
(2호선 신촌역 6번 출구 바로 앞) 5F 숲속의언어

코딩어학원
CodingLanguageSchool.com

PART II

파이썬 중급:
Blob world pygame 만들기

처음 코딩할 때 영어 speech를 들으면서 실습하는 습관을 길들이는 것은 매우 중요합니다! 대한민국 모든 청소년들이 너도 나도 코딩영어로 무장해 담대하게 세상에 나아가게 해 드리는 것이 저희 목표입니다. 저희가 개발한 이 자기주도학습법이 왜 우수할까요?

1. 코딩은 영어로 만든 용어요, 문법이라 영어로 들었을 때 가장 쉽게 이해가 가게 되어 있다.
2. 실습을 해서 결과가 맞게 나오면 영어가 들렸다는 얘기니깐, 혼자서도 학습이 절로 된다.
3. 정 이해가 안 되고 실습 결과가 계속 다르게 나오면, 그땐 코딩영어의 도움을 받으면 된다.

유튜브에서 강의 제목과 'sentdex'로 검색하심 Harrison Kinsley의 원본 비디오가 나옵니다. LC training(6:20). 괄호 안의 숫자는 거기 비디오가 시작되는 지점을 말합니다.

1 Introduction

드디어 중급 과정에 들어왔습니다.

지난 한달 간에 배웠던 초급은 목표가 Let's just make this work! 였다면, 이제 중급에선 목표가 Break these down to the following three hallmarks/trademarks입니다:

1. efficiency, scaling – scales well as your project grows. Otherwise, you'll pay off and they call it technical debt.

2. maintainability, readability – issues how easily we can understand it. functions, classes, methods usage. get to the point as the project grows.

3. modularity – you use this in other projects of your own or other people can make use of the code that you're writing. So you should make something that's extremely generalizable.

the life of a software engineer, ... much later 에 관한 comic한 웹진 사진이 하나 올랐습니다. 처음의 각오입니다: Clean slate, solid foundations. This time I will build things the right way. 각오와는 달리 시간이 지나고 나서 보면: Oh my, I've done it again haven't I? 우린 언제나 ~ this is just kind of gluing things together only. 라는 생각이 들게 마련입니다. 이 그림이 a kind of modular 하다고요? But it's difficult for this kind of project to scale!!!

maintainability를 지키기 위해 나온 다큐멘트가 PEP8 - Style Guide for Python 입니다. 참고하면 좋아요. 보다 나은 지침용 다큐멘트로는 전 시간에 본 >>>import this ... the zen of python 도 있어요.

앞으로 우린 중급 과정에서 built-in things: generators, list comprehension; standard libraries - multiprocessing; object oriented programming - one of the best ways to make modular codes 등을 배우게 될 것입니다.

Now with intermediate Python programming i kind of break these down There's kind of like three hallmarks or trademarks of intermediate Python programming and That is one it's efficient and it scales well because as you grow a project and if the project is successful it needs to be able to scale Otherwise you're gonna have to go back and pay off a bunch of what's called technical debt basically So you want to be able to scale really well Also along those lines The second thing is just maintainability So a lot of this is just readability and how easily we can understand it but also just how well you write your functions and classes and methods and stuff like this that allows you to actually grow over time and improve it because a lot of times you're just going to get to the point where as the project grows and you want to add new things or change things it can become just a huge spiderweb mess nastiness Then finally the third thing is just modularity and so The idea here is that when you we make something your goal should be that maybe you want to use this in other projects of your own or maybe Other people can make use of the code that you're writing So you want to make something that's extremely generalizable that should be the goal and that's actually really hard to do and if you're not always thinking about that it's really easy to take the short route and sacrifice modularity but also sacrifice maintainability and even efficiency But for the most part scaling and efficiency is more of like a knowledge thing you just need to know how to do it as apposed to maintainability and modularity that's more of like a mindset that you really need to have So one thing i always like to show i've shown this picture a few times before but i think it's a really good one is this kind of comic and the idea is that you know you start with a clean slate and then you build your first project and that's just this simple house And then overtime as the project grows you want to add these other little things to it and as time goes on it just gets way out of hand everything's just kind of pieced together There was no thought about i mean obviously i guess this is kind of modular But it's really difficult for this kind of project to scale when you're just kind of gluing things together And again it's more like a mindset when you're writing things

2) String operations

string data를 처리하다 보면, concatenation은 어떻게 하지? formatting은 어떻게 하지? 하는 의문이 생깁니다. 가장 기본이 되는 기능이기도 하지만, 이 두 개의 function 용법을 알고나면 앞으론 string을 갖고선 얼마든지 scaling이 가능한 코딩역량을 갖추게 되십니다. join()과 format()입니다.

```python
names = ['Jeff', 'Gary', 'Jill', 'Samantha']
for name in names:
      print('Hello there, ' + name)
      print(' '.join(['Hello there,', name]))
print(', '.join(names))          # scales better

import os
location_of_files = 'C: \\Users\\USER\\Desktop\\Intermediate-
Tutorials'
file_name = 'example.txt'
print(location_of_files + '\\' + file_name)
with open(os.path.join(location_of_files, file_name)) as f:
      print(f.read())

who = 'Gary'
how_many = 12
# Gary bought 12 apples today!
print(who, 'bought', how_many, 'apples today!')
print('{} bought {} apples today!'.format(who, how_many))   #
the correct way of string formatting
```

It's the same thing but if you ask me the first one is just so much readable and i'm not really sure that it's worth the performance gain here And as Python changes overtime these are things like subtle things like these There really are going to change by Python even version sometimes So in some senses this they might be like the difference is probably just extremely negligible you'll get away with it But the difference is when say you've got a list of strings or really anything and you want to just print them out as a string print that list as a string of course you could do string names and just print that But let's say instead you actually want to just print the list of the names as a string So that might look something like let me just comment this out whoops comment this out and that might look like whoops not again um We will join just as a comma dot join and then names is a list so we're fine Let's run that and in fact let's do comma space There we go so now we've got Jeff Garry Jill Samantha okay So that that works Is it easily readable? If you know how join works then sure it's readable But if you don't know how join works that's not readable at all But when it comes to concatenating strings join is preferable when you're joining more than two strings Some people will argue that maybe it's more than like some number of strings like when the processing changes But i think it is a general rule of thumb if you're going to concatenate and truly concatenate because actually what we're doing here we are concatenated but we're still actually kind of doing the wrong thing in both of these examples I'll show you the right things soon enough But probably this isn't even the right way to go about it But if you're concatenating two or more than two not two two or more so basically all concatenation no If you're in concatenating more than two strings you probably should be using join purely because it's going to scale better It's going to use less processing

3 Argparse for CLI

coding할 때엔 약간씩 미세조정이 필요한 부분이 나옵니다. 이런 건 주 editor IDE 와는 별도로 가볍게 기능시험 해 보는 용도로 CLI command line interface 가 자주 쓰입니다. 실습에선 CLI 환경에서 arguments를 parse 해 operation을 수행하게 해 주는 argparse.ArgumentParser( )란 메소드를 활용해 사칙연산 응용을 만들어 냈습니다. help 기능까지 들어간 완벽한 작품이 몇 안 되는 코딩으로 가능하다는 것을 보여 줍니다.

```python
import argparse
import sys

def main():
    parser = argparse.ArgumentParser()
    parser.add_argument('--x', type=float, default=1.0,
help='What is the first number?')
    parser.add_argument('--y', type=float, default=1.0,
help='What is the second number?')
    parser.add_argument('--operation', type=str,
default='add', help='What operation? (add, sub, mul, or div)')
    args = parser.parse_args()
    sys.stdout.write(str(calc(args))) #system out to the
console

def calc(args):
    if args.operation == 'add':
        return args.x + args.y
    elif args.operation == 'sub':
        return args.x - args.y
    elif args.operation == 'mul':
```

```python
        return args.x * args.y
    elif args.operation == 'div':
        return args.x / args.y


if __name__ == '__main__':
main()
```

So let's convert this to command line interface So the first thing that we're going to do is we're gonna import argparse and we're gonna import sys so then we're gonna do define main and then main is where we're going to actually build the arguments themselves As you might guess from the name argparse it's an argument parser surprise! So what we're going to do is we're going to define the parser and the parser is equal to argparse dot argument parser One quick note on um PEP 8 when i see the following argparse ArgumentParser i am i can assume ArgumentParser is a class and parser equals is an object of that ArgmentParser class How do i know? Because of the Studley case Again that's just that's one reason why you want to sometimes adhere to PEP 8 because it's clear to me immediately when i know like that's the name of that okay it's a parser object it's not some sort of function that's returning some sort of value that we're calling parser Moving along parser dot add argument again because we know parser is an object we know add argument's a method that doesn't make much sense to you right Now it will soon because we're going to be talking about Object Oriented Programming soon moving on The first argument we'll add is just dash dash x that's going to take the place of this x parameter So that's the name of it The type we're gonna say is a float then we're gonna say default equals 1.0 and then we're going to come down and we're going to add some help and the help is just like a some sort of string that's going to explain what this is so we're just gonna say what is the first number ... So those are the arguments Now we're going to say the args is equal to parser dot parse the args and then we're just going to sys dot s standard output dot write the string version of calc args okay So this is all necessary to do with argparse and then the system out The reason why we're doing this is So the output will actually come to the to the console itself In many cases you could just use print But there's going to be times when actually you need to do a system out Because otherwise you're just not going to see it

4 List Comp & Generators

range function은 python 2에선 not a generator였다. it does store the entire list in memory. as the result when it's big number, it will blowout your memory. 그러다 이제 python 3에 와선 generator가 되었고, it doesn't store in the memory. range(5)라 하면, it generates a stream in the range of 0 to five, produces 0, 1, 2, 3, 4, builds and saves that list to a variable. list comprehension은 xyz = [i for i in range(5)], generator expression은 xyz = (i for i in range(i)) 라고 코딩한다. 전자는

```
xyz = []
for i in range(5):
    xyz.append(i)
```

후자는

```
for i in xyz:
    print(i)
```

해 보면 둘이 동일하게 [0, 1, 2, 3, 4]를 출력하는 걸 볼 수 있다. 이 둘은 전자는 메모리를 잡아먹고, 후자는 프로세스 타임을 잡아먹는다는 특성을 갖고 있다. 아래와 같이 몇 차례 number를 바꿔가며 실습을 통해 그 현상을 지켜볼 수 있었다.

```
xyz = [i for i in range(50000000)]  # list comprehension -
loads in a list memory
    print('done')      # ... it took 3.8 secs
```

```
xyz = (i for i in range(50000000))  # generator expression -
creates an object
      print(xyz)          # ... it took only 0.1 secs
------------------------------------------------------------------
done
<generator object <genexpr> at 0x000001E91BACBAC0>
[Finished in 3.9s]
```

One of the most common generators that you've probably been using is range So when you say for i in range of five this does not generate a list of 0 1 2 3 4 it's a generator and it generates a stream in the range of 0 to 5 which is producing 0 1 2 3 4 so But it doesn't do that and save it all into memory as apposed to say list comprehension or a list that actually obviously would store that into memory So in Python 2 range actually isn't a generator and it does store that entire list in the memory which is why if you in Python 3 you can get away with saying like i equals range this that's okay You're going to be just fine when you do that right We can do that real quick ok boom it's already done all right But in Python 2 if you run that code it's gonna be like plurr ~ like it's just not gonna happen and you're gonna have to close out a Python okay so Because it's generating a list and it's just going to blow your memory so generator Now fundamentally we'll i have to keep hitting this point as we go through this entire course really But list comprehension or a list is going to be faster but it's going to use your memory right It's going to use your RAM to store that list and that's why it's faster It's already loaded boom it's in memory Generators on the other hand are going to be slower but they're not going to use as much memory and slower is like with an asterisk Because building a list actually like when it comes time to build and save that list to a variable that can actually sometimes be a pretty time intensive process so Actually sometimes generators are faster But in most like raw cases the generator is going to be slower it's just not going to blow out your memory

5) More list comp and generators

어떤 numbers' list에 5로 나누어서 remainder가 0로 나오는(5로 나누어지는) numbers를 찾아내는 기능을 하는 function을 하나 만들어 냈다. 그 이름을 div_by_five(num)라 했다.

generator에선, xyz = (i for i in input_list if div_by_five(i))

[print(i) for i in xyz]라고 one line of for loops로 출력해 낸다.

list comprehension에선, xyz = [i for i in input_list if div_by_file(i)]

역시 [print(i) for i in xyz] 라고 one line of for loops로 출력해 낸다.

여기 embedded 개념을 소개한다. one line of two for loops다.

전자는 list comprehension, 후자는 generator다:

```
[[print(i, ii) for ii in range(5)] for i in range(5)]
for i in range(5):
        for ii in range(5):
                print(i, ii)

xyz = (((i, ii) for ii in range(5)) for i in range(5))
print(xyz)
for i in xyz:
        for ii in i:
                print(ii)
----------------------------------------------------------------
0 0
0 1
0 2
0 3
0 4
1 0
```

```
...
4 4
<generator object <genexpr> at 0x000002DE18B7BE40>
(0, 0)
(0, 1)
(0, 2)
(0, 3)
(0, 4)
(1, 0)
...
(4, 4)
```

There's an old saying: with big list comprehensions you would run out of memory, with big generators you'll run out of time.

끝으로 tip 하나 더.

```
xyz = (print(i) for i in range(5)) # this generates print object
for i in xyz:      # in order to print that object,
      i      # it's enough by putting just the print object only
----------------------------------------------------------------
0
1
2
3
4
```

So that's xyz Now what we can say is for i in xyz print i whoops there we go so what it's doing now is xyz is a generator and we're iterating over that generator and sure enough it went through the input list and found just what was divisible by 5 What else could we have done rather than for i and xyz print i? Well we could say print i for i in xyz Could just done that pull this over see same thing So a lot of times people actually call list comprehension one line of for loops Because that's basically what they're there they're using list comprehension not necessary necessarily for a list comprehension's sake they're literally just doing it to put it all on one line And so you'll hear people call them one-liner for loops myself included Just depending on what you're trying to do So anyway so you can do that Now could we make a generator out of it or can we do this comprehension with this? Absolutely literally all we're doing is this and then this Now remember up here if we were to print xyz we would never have actually had an answer So when you're printing i for i and xyz your machine is not needing to load the entire list because it's not a list But in this case it wouldn't need to load an entire list into memory because it's actually iterating over a generator So you're saving your memory but it's slower ish what's up Because sometimes building a list is actually intensive So now we're going to say xyz equals i for i in this So again just so we are totally clear i'll print xyz here we're redefining xyz here i'll print xyz here save and run that I don't know why it keeps popping up over there Anyway we get it xyz is actually a generator object and then here it's truly a list But we can iterate over them all the same So we could in theory just do this copy/ paste run same thing We're just iterating over that list

6 Timeit

앞의 두 단원에 이어서 계속되는 이슈입니다. list comprehensions과 generator expressions 간에 소요되는 running time을 측정해서 비교해 볼 수가 있는데, 이 때에 사용하는 것이 timeit module입니다.

timeit measures the amount of time it takes for a certain snippet of code to run.

간단히 '1+3'이란 a string of python code로 number variable을 500,000 그리고 50,000,000회 숫자를 주어서 수행해 보았더니 각기 0.006243, 0.621717 secs가 걸렸다고 나옵니다.

```
import timeit
print(timeit.timeit('1+3', number=50000000))
```

자, 본론에 들어가서 list comp와 generators 간에 비교입니다. 역시 앞 강에서 사용했던 div_by_five(num) function을 활용합니다.

```
import timeit
# xyz = (i for i in input_list if dev_by_five(i))
# xyz = [i for i in input_list if dev_by_five(i)]
print(timeit.timeit('''input_list = range(100)

def dev_by_five(num):
        if num % 5 == 0:
                return True
        else:
                return False

xyz = [i for i in input_list if dev_by_five(i)]
for i in xyz:
```

```
        x = i''', number=500000))

# xyz = [] # the logic of the above list comp how it works
# for i in input_list:
#       if div_by_five(i):
#             xyz.append(i)
--------------------------------------------------------------------
7.570000100000001
[Finished in 7.7s]
```

Another thing that we could do is compare the following so what if we wanted to compare this is getting messy So let's first write the code and then we'll time it below So we've got div by five we've got the generator expression up here Let us time the iteration I'm going to comment this out for now I'm not going to see it right this moment Let's time how long it takes to do for i in xyz print i So let's run this code so the creation of a generator in the iteration through that generator So we'll copy this will comment it out paste it run it And in fact it's going to print it out oh no ha ~ okay Let's just define a variable Let's just say x equals i It's like printing out to my console That's not on the same screen okay it's fascinating it just it went Now that tells you how slow printing the console is okay Let's try it one more time just cleaning up things okay So this was with the generator and then an iteration through just going off of my memory This is pretty close to how long it took for us just to build the list Now let's do list comprehension So we just changed these two things So list comprehension is slightly faster not by a whole lot But let's add some numbers here and okay So this will be list comprehension How many do we add? So it should take about nine seconds probably i shouldn't have done it for that long But while we're waiting let's just change this to a generator okay nine point four seconds And we'll run it one more time So that was for list comprehension now we'll see how long it might take for a generator But again the whole point of a generator isn't to be fast it's to not use memory But that time it appears to actually in all the other cases it was not faster because remember this was the generator this was list comprehension This is list comprehension this is a generator Interesting but in that case it was faster

7 Enumerate

초급 12강 diagonal winner 알고리즘에서 우린 enumerate() built-in function을 활용해 game_board를 만들어 내 본 적이 있습니다.

it's going to return a tuple containing basically the count along the way and then the object itself or the item itself that you were iterating over.

```python
example = ['left', 'right', 'up', 'down']
for i in range(len(example)):
        print(i, example[i])
```

pretty much anytime you're going to say for i in range of a length of something you're probably doing it wrong. this is not the right way to go about it. let's fix it like the following:

```python
for i, j in enumerate(example):
        print(i, j) # prints counter, item value of the tuple
```

그리고 우린 dictionary data type으로도 전환해 내어 보았습니다.

```python
new_dict = dict(enumerate(example)) # this case produces
dictionary dataset
print(new_dict) # prints key made by count, item value of the
dictionary
[print(i, j) for i, j in enumerate(new_dict)] # i is enumerate
count, j is the key value of dictionary
```

```
[print(i, j) for i, j in enumerate(example)] # i is enumerate
count, j is item value of tuple
another_dict = {'left':'<','right':'>','up':'^','down':'v',}
[print(i,j) for i,j in enumerate(another_dict)] # prints
enumerate count, first item value only
----------------------------------------------------------------
0 left
1 right
2 up
3 down
{0: 'left', 1: 'right', 2: 'up', 3: 'down'}
0 0
1 1
2 2
3 3
0 left
1 right
2 up
3 down
0 left
1 right
2 up
3 down
[Finished in 138ms]
```

First let's say we're just going to say an example equals left right up and down and what we're going to say is we'll just do will do for i in range len example print i example i So this is an example of code that you might find yourself writing to produce the following like Basically any time you find yourself or i would say most of the time i'm trying to think of an example where i've not been screwing up when i do this But pretty much anytime you're going to say for i in range of a length of something you're probably doing it wrong okay So just keep that in mind i've done it probably No i know i've done in some of the tutorials for sure just because like i just never use enumerate I just don't think about it But lately in my own code i've been trying to use enumerate just because it exists and you should do it so Anyways this is not the right way to go about it Instead what you should say is something like this for i j in enumerate example print i j I'll print the other one just to do it i guess but as you can see this one ended here or this the first one this is the second one Exact same output just a little cleaner um it makes a little bit more sense It's the way it's supposed to be you're also not doing like this range len nonsense You just don't need to so don't do it So that's one example of enumerate for most people that's probably all you need to do You can use enumerate over a dictionary and a lot of other iterables I would show you a dictionary You can go to the sample code if you really want to see it But it's basically the exact same thing as we just did here

8 Zip

zip takes elements from multiple iterables and aggregates them into one where we basically share the index value.

remember that we learned in the previous class: () parentheses, [] square brackets, {} curly brackets. in python we call it tuple, list, dictionary data type respectively.

```
x = [1, 2, 3, 4]
y = [7, 6, 2, 1]
z = ['a', 'b', 'c', 'd']
for a, b, c in zip(x,y,z):
        print(a,b)
print(zip(x,y,z))           # object only
print(list(zip(x,y,z)))         # three iterables
print(dict(zip(x,y)))   # two iterables
[print(a,b,c) for a,b,c in zip(x,y,z)]
[print(x,y) for x,y in zip(x,y)]
print(x)     # not overwritten
[print(a,b) for a,b in zip(x,y)]
print(a)     # overwritten
for a,b in zip(x,y):
        print(a,b)
print(a)     # overwritten
for x,y in zip(x,y):
        print(x,y)
print(x)     # overwritten
------------------------------------------------------------
1 7
2 6
3 2
```

```
4 1
<zip object at 0x000001FAAABB4AC0>
[(1, 7, 'a'), (2, 6, 'b'), (3, 2, 'c'), (4, 1, 'd')]
{1: 7, 2: 6, 3: 2, 4: 1}
1 7 a
2 6 b
3 2 c
4 1 d
1 7
2 6
3 2
4 1
[1, 2, 3, 4]
1 7
2 6
3 2
4 1
4
1 7
2 6
3 2
4 1
4
1 7
2 6
3 2
4 1
4
[Finished in 242ms]
```

Sometimes it might be tempting to take this line and instead maybe we're going to we could write this we could print x y and we'll just do x y for x y in zip x y This seems good right so we'll run that and we get what we expected and then later on If we decide we wanted to print x Is x what we expected? X to be 1 2 3 4 yep That is what we thought x was going to be Because we know that these are temporary variables right in a for loop but hmm Is that the case? so what if we said for a b or print a b for a b in zip x y and then we print a after that So there's these variables okay we get a is not defined But what if we did the same list comprehension just in a typical for loop Well we would say for a b in zip x y print a b same thing i'm just going to comment this out But it's the same it's going to produce the same output anyway But see what happens on the print a Huh looks like that a was stored what's more is instead of before when we said in the list comprehension example for x y or print x y for x y in zip x y we recognize that these were just temporary values they weren't actually being stored But in the for loop they are stored So when you say print for x y and zip x y this will work It's going to work it's going to be fine No one's going to loose their shirt But when we go to print x afterwards let me just comment this out It's overwritten x y so you might find yourself in a scenario where you're not using list comprehension you're writing a simple for loop And because you've gotten away with this in list comp you think you're going to get away with it here but you don't And then you decide that you're going to iterate again like for x or for i in x or something like this you're going to continue using that x variable and it's just not going to work So just remember that in list comp these values aren't going to overwrite our original variables and in fact they're not even stored after the loop But or after the full iteration is complete but in regular for loop that value is stored and it's going to overwrite your old variables So if you get in the habit of just using the same variable names as you're iterating over it it's probably a bad idea because you're gonna you might find yourself in a situation like this

9 Writing generators

```python
[i for i in range(5)]    # list comprehension
(i for i in range(5))    # generator expression

def simple_gen():                    # a simple generator
     yield 'Oh'
     yield 'hello'
     yield 'there'

for i in simple_gen():
     print(i)

CORRECT_COMBO = (3, 6, 1)

# for loop
found_combo = False
for c1 in range(10):
     if found_combo:
          break
          for c2 in range(10):
               if found_combo:
                    break
               for c3 in range(10):
                    if (c1, c2, c3) == CORRECT_COMBO:
                         print('Found the combo:
                    {}'.format((c1, c2, c3)))
                         found_combo = True
                         break
                    print(c1,c2,c3)
```

```
# generator
def combo_gen():
      for c1 in range(10):
            for c2 in range(10):
                  for c3 in range(10):
                        yield(c1, c2, c3)      # yields a stream of
                  tuple dataset
for (c1, c2, c3) in combo_gen():
      print(c1, c2, c3)
      if (c1, c2, c3) == CORRECT_COMBO:
            print('Found the combo: {}'.format((c1, c2, c3)))
            break
---------------------------------------------------------------
Oh
hello
there
0 0 0
0 0 1
0 0 2
0 0 3
0 0 4
...
3 5 7
3 5 8
3 5 9
3 6 0
Found the combo: (3, 6, 1)
0 0 0
0 0 1
0 0 2
0 0 3
0 0 4
...
3 5 7
3 5 8
3 5 9
3 6 0
3 6 1
Found the combo: (3, 6, 1)
[Finished in 150ms]
```

Rather than using for loops what we might do is let's make generator So instead let me just make some space here instead We're gong to say define combo gen and then it's going to be basically everything that we just saw But we're going to just do for c1 in range 10 for c2 and range 10 for c3 in range 10 yield c1, c2, c3 okay so we're going to yield these and that's our generator Now what we're going to do is iterate over the generator So for c1 c2 c3 in combo-gen because that's our generator So what do we know about the generator? We know that it's ret it does not return things I was even said it returns It yields things in a streaming and that stream can be ceased either through logic in the generator itself or we can stop it So for c1 c2 c3 in combo generator what are we gonna do? We first of all we can print just so we can see it c1 c2 c3 and then if this c1 c2 c3 if that equals our correct combo then we will this print then we found the combo and we're just going to break boom one break statement oh c1 c2 c3 we'll just do that good run it It's running notice it's a little there it is okay found the combo 3 6 & 1 here it is Found the combo and notice we didn't even make it to this print statement Everything is done The generator is no longer generating anything we got our answer So in this case we were able to actually breakout with a single break Now in terms of line count i'm pretty sure this only saves us like two lines in reality But if you ask me this is a lot cleaner looking much more simple and it was much easier to actually use our logic and we got to use a generator which wasn't wasting our memory In this case this was a really simple task test But in many cases you might find yourself trying to do something like this and just just getting outrageous like we did here like This is just ugly

10 Multi-processing

Why multiprocessing? your cpu does not get fully utilized depending on how many cores you have will max out at about 16 percent of the cpu because of the GIL.

Global Interpreter Lock - memory management safeguard

there's a lot of infra structure built with the assumption that we have that memory management safeguard of GIL.

what multiprocessing is going to allow you to do is to utilize multiple processes.

you can write a python program that does something and you can run it and it will use a whole cpu cores you have, such as six cores. cpus equals cores.

what the multiprocessing library allows you to do or makes easy for you is launching separate python processes that don't necessarily talk to each other.

```python
import multiprocessing
'''
def spawn(num):
    print('Spawned! {}'.format(num))
if __name__ == '__main__':
    for i in range(50):
        p = multiprocessing.Process(target=spawn,
    args=(i, ))
        p.start()
        # p.join()         # waits until prior task ends
'''
def spawn(num, num2):
    print('Spawned! {} {}'.format(num,num2))
if __name__ == '__main__':
    for i in range(500):
```

```
        p = multiprocessing.Process(target=spawn,
args=(i,i+1))
        p.start()
# p.join() # this manages tasks on scheduled
        # without this, cpu doesn't wait the other tasks
        # spending up to over 90%, up to 100% several times
```

```
Spawned! 0 1
Spawned! 1 2
Spawned! 2 3
Spawned! 5 6
Spawned! 3 4
Spawned! 8 9
Spawned! 13 14
Spawned! 7 8
Spawned! 4 5
...
Spawned! 484 485
Spawned! 496 497
Spawned! 490 491
Spawned! 481 482
Spawned! 498 499
Spawned! 495 496
Spawned! 497 498
[Finished in 12.3s]
```

First of all we're going to import multiprocessing it is a part of your standard library so everybody has it and then we're going to define a really simple function this is just going to be define we're going to call it spawn and then all spawn is going to do is print spawn with a capital S Then what we're going to do is we're going to do if name equals main and if this was ever necessary it's necessary in multiprocessing again this just makes it So the whatever's under here will only run when it's the script itself that's being run And so if the script is being called by something else it won't run So if name equals main we're going to run something and that's something we're going to say is for i in range of however many you want Let's just say 5 and what we're gonna say now is p for the process it will be equal to multiprocessing dot process So this just allows us to spawn a process and we're going to say the target is going to be just the function and that's going to be spawn So that's our process then we're going to say p dot start that starts the process p dot join basically this is waiting for the process to be complete So now what i want to do is open up a command window or terminal if you're in Linux Open up a command window and what we're going to do is call this script So you could you can run it in idle or whatever But it's not gonna we're not going to see the print out So i'm going to run it in a shell so we can actually see her in command prompt So i first of all need to specify the full path to Python you probably don't i just have multiple Python versions so i need to be explicit and then i'm going to say 10 period and then it's multiprocessing tutorial dot py good so we'll run it and then we see spawn spawn spawn okay cool Now you probably won't see it in this case but if i pull up the task manager so let me pull that up and wait for you it's taking a while when it finally comes up go to your background processes So you should get this if you see like this hit more details and then you'll scroll down and then basically it's alphabetical so LMNOP so around here is where we should see the Python processes We're not seeing any right now but it i go and rerun this we should see it yeah There's a couple of Python processes momentarily

파이썬 프로그래밍 **코딩영어**

(11) Getting process values

can retrieve information from our processes

can get information back from your processes

how to actually retrieve a return value from our process

```python
from multiprocessing import Pool
def job(num):
        return num * 2


if __name__ == '__main__':
        p = Pool(processes=20) # how many processes we want on
pool
        data = p.map(job, range(20)) # what's job? there's a
definition on the above
        data2 = p.map(job, [5,2])     # .map() needs two
arguments – method, any type of iterable
        p.close()
print(data)
print(data2)


# a parameter is the variable which is part of the method's
signature (method declaration).
# an argument is an expression used when calling the method.
-------------------------------------------------------------------
[0, 2, 4, 6, 8, 10, 12, 14, 16, 18, 20, 22, 24, 26, 28, 30, 32, 34, 36, 38]
[10, 4]
[Finished in 560ms]
```

First we're going to start by from multiprocessing we're going to import pool and what pool does is just allows us to create a pool of process workers Then we're going to say is define job job will take a parameter number and for now we'll just return num times two really complicated job then again we'll have if name equals main and if that's the case we're going to say p now equals to actually pool and then we'll say how many processes we want let's just say 20 and then we're going to say data equals p dot map and then we're going to map the job itself to some sort of iterable it can be any iterable So for example it could be a generator so we can say range 20 and then we're gonna say p dot close and then let's print data And what we're going to get back data from mapping is actually going to be its own iterable It'll be a list of values from 0 to 20 times 2 so it should be 0 2 4 8 and so on Let's see it sure enough that's what we get 0 to the roo~~ all the way up to 38 So that's just a really quick example of how we're retrieving information from our processes Now there are ways to retrieve processes without mapping a function to an iterable But real quick let me just show you like we could do the foll like it can just be like a list like this right 2 4 6 8 but it also could just be like a single value so you could just do 4 right and you get returned back in 8 or it could be a string and this does something to a string and so on So you can do mapping with just single value and like i said There are other ways without doing mapping but i feel like with mapping it just makes sense because you can either map a single value if you really wanted to I' not sure why you would have a single value to a single function with in need multiprocessing but there you go But in most cases you're going to use some sort of iterable in this case we've got just 4 There's nothing to it but you can put through a generator or a list or whatever you want So you can do that but you can also do like the following So you could say we'll do range 5 here and then we can copy this and then if you wanted to do something else like maybe it's a different function where you only have the one function but say you want to do a different function with a different process We'll just say data 2 it was that data 2 you can of course do this as well

(12) Multi-processing spider

multiprocessing along with beautifulsoup as an example of when multi-processing could be advantageous

concept 1. a spider might have multiple subtasks but the main task of a spider is to go to a website, finds all of the links on that website and then goes to all of those links and just slowly spiderwebs out on to the entire interwebs.

```
pip install beautifulsoup4, lxml

from multiprocessing import Pool
import bs4 as bs
import random
import requests
import string


# Beautiful Soup is a Python library for pulling data out of
HTML and XML files.
# It works with your favorite parser to provide idiomatic ways
of navigating, searching,
# and modifying the parse tree. It commonly saves programmers
hours or days of work.

def random_starting_url():
    starting =
''.join(random.SystemRandom().choice(string.ascii_lowercase)
for _ in range(3))
    url = ''.join(['http://', starting, '.com'])
    return url
```

```
# url = random_starting_url()
# print(url)

def handle_local_links(url,link):
        if link.startswith('/'):        # url에 이어서 '/'가 나온다면 그건
하위 디렉트리 link
                return ''.join([url,link])   # url과 그 directory
        link를 붙여서 값을 돌려 준다
        else:
                return link       # 그 외에는, 그냥 원래 link 값만 돌려
        준다
def get_links(url):
        try:
                resp = requests.get(url)
                soup = bs.BeautifulSoup(resp.text, 'lxml')      #
        pulls data out of HTML and XML
                body = soup.body
                links = [link.get('href') for link in
        body.find_all('a')]     # all 'a'에서 'href'를 찾아
                links = [handle_local_links(url,link) for link in
        links]     # '/'가 따라 나오면 그 하위 링크를 붙여서
                links = [str(link.encode("ascii")) for link in links]
                # ascii 형태로 링크 값을 돌려 준다
                return links


        except TypeError as e:
                print(e)
                print('Got a TypeError, probably got a None that we
        tried to iterate over')
                return []
        except IndexError as e:
                print(e)
                print('We probably did not find any useful links,
        returning enpty list')
                return []
        except AttributeError as e:
                print(e)
                print('Likely got None for links, so we are throwing
        this')
```

```
            return []
        except Exception as e:
            print(str(e))
            # log this error
            return []


def main():
    how_many = 50
    p = Pool(processes=how_many)
    parse_us = [random_starting_url() for _ in
range(how_many)]   # 세 자리 url을 찾아 나온 걸로
    data = p.map(get_links, [link for link in parse_us])        #
spider map으로 다시 찾아 나온 links를 list data에다 담았다가
    data = [url for url_list in data for url in url_list]        #
url_list 안의 url_list들을 모두 하나의 list data로 모아서
    p.close()

    with open('urls.txt','w') as f:     # 그 값을 별도의 파일에다
담아낸다.
        f.write(str(data))


if __name__ == '__main__':
    main()
# look up the https://pythonprogramming.net/introduction-
scraping.../
# held just before this intermediate lectures.
--------------------------------------------------------------------
C:\Users\USER\Desktop\Intermediate-Tutorials>python
intermediate12.py
HTTPConnectionPool(host='bxw.com', port=80): Max retries
exceeded with url: / (Caused by
...
NewConnectionError('<urllib3.connection.HTTPConnection
object at 0x000001EF099842B0>: Failed to establish a new
connection: [Errno 11001] getaddrinfo failed'))
'NoneType' object has no attribute 'find_all'
Likely got None for links, so we are throwing this
...
```

```
HTTPConnectionPool(host='iyi.com', port=80): Max retries
exceeded with url: / (Caused by
NewConnectionError('<urllib3.connection.HTTPConnection
object at 0x000001F8F1590B00>: Failed to establish a new
connection: [WinError 10060] 연결된 구 성원으로부터 응답이 없어
연결하지 못했거나, 호스트로부터 응답이 없어 연결이 끊어졌습니다'))
-----------------------------------------------------------------
["b'#main'", "b'https://www.linde.com/'",
 "b'http://boc.com/en/about-boc/'",
 "b'http://boc.com/en/careers/'",
 "b'https://www.boconline.co.uk/shop/LogonForm...'",
 "b'https://www.boconline.co.uk/.../store-finder/index.html'",
 "b'https://www.boconline.co.uk/shop/en/uk/customer-information'",
 "b'http://boc.com/en/'", "b'http://boc.com/en/'",
 "b'http://boc.com/en/'", "b'http://boc.com/en/index.html'",
 "b'http://boc.com/en/shop-online/index.html'",
 ...
 "b'https://www.instagram.com/ellenbrussdesign/?hl=en'",
 "b'https://www.etsy.com/shop/HermannAndSmalls?ref'",
 "b'https://goo.gl/maps/YDGd4wFyqTE2'",
 "b'https://ebd.com/accessibility/'"]
```

What we're doing here is we're saying parse us This is going to be a list of urls basically a list three character urls and then we're coming down here from basically this will be the data that we basically the same as what we did in the previous tutorial where we're the you know the return was like a list of 0 2 4 6 8 and so on This time it's a mapping and it's gonna be lists of urls that we get for all of the links in parse us You might be able to guess already that what we're going to do is parse us this starting value is a list of urls What are we getting back from here with get links a list of urls Thus this could be a process that just recurse infinitely But not yet because data is a list of lists So what we're going to say is now data is going to be equal to url for url list in data for url in url list How is that for list comprehension what is that doing So for every url in each of the mini url lists and then for each of the mini url lists in all of the urls that we have which is data We're saying what we want to do is now have a new list which is just those contents So this is a way of taking a list of lists and taking the data from each of those lists in the lists and putting into a single list fantastic

(13) Intro to OOP

concept 1. the purpose of object-oriented programming is to create objects and these objects have attributes and then they also have methods so the attributes are like characteristics and the methods are basically actions or ways for us to be able to actually interact with these objects.

'''

concept 2. why do we need to create a class and the object?

in order to make the code sources:

1. scalable ... 확장해서 쓸 수 있게

2. maintainable ... 유지 보수에 편리하게

3. modulable ... 쉽게 가져다 쓸 수 있게

4. interactive ... object 간에 서로 소통할 수 있게

concept 3. what's the characteristics of OOP?

the answers are:

1. modularity 이식가능성

2. inheritance 상속성

3. abstract 추상(抽象)성

'''

```
pip install pygame
class Blob:
    def __init__(self, color):     # whenever this object is
created, init method just runs
        self.x = random.randrange(0, WIDTH)
        self.y = random.randrange(0, HEIGHT)
        self.size = random.randrange(4,8)
        self.color = color
```

concept 4. What these arguments do is self just this instance. It's this object instance that we're going to be able to share throughout the entire object here. So through out the entire class the things that we define is like self dot something like to start. We're going to have maybe self dot color. Since we're passing color here that's going to have some sort of value. We're going to set that to be whatever color is. So now this object is an attribute of this object right and we can reference it in the definition of the class anywhere and in another method. It doesn't have to be in the init method. So we can reference this elsewhere using self dot. But then outside of this when we actually do create the object and save it to a variable name, we do that variable name dot color and that is how we can access the color attribute.

```python
def move(self):
    self.move_x = random.randrange(-1,2)
    self.move_y = random.randrange(-1,2)
    self.x += self.move_x
    self.y += self.move_y

    if self.x < 0: self.x = 0
    elif self.x > WIDTH: self.x = WIDTH
    if self.y < 0: self.y = 0
    elif self.y > HEIGHT: self.y = HEIGHT
```

First of all the thing that creates an object is a class So we're going to define we'll just start by defining a class and we're going to call this class Blob and what we're going to do at least to start is we're going to be creating a sort of blob world that consists of an environment that these blobs are living within And the blobs will interact with each other but also just the general environment that can do things in the environment But first we need to define what this blob object actually is What are its attributes and what are things that this blob can actually do So just class Blob: and you're good to go And right away we're going to define the first our first method and what we're going to do is we're going to define the dunder itter oh not dunder itter haha dunder init method dunder itter will come eventally But dunder init is the first we're gonna do and we're gonna pass self and then we're gonna pass color So what these arguments do is self is just this this instance It's this object instance that we're going to be able to share throughout the entire object here So throughout the entire class the things that we define is like self dot something like to start we're gonna have maybe self dot color Since we're passing color here That's gonna have some sort of value We're gonna set that to be whatever color is So now this object this is an attribute of this object right and we can reference it in the definition of the class anywhere and in another method it doesn't have to be in the init method So we can reference this elsewhere using self dot but then outside of this when we actually do create the object and save it to a variable name we do that variable name dot color and that is how we can access the color attribute You'll see that more as when we get there But self is just you can pick any name for self but self is just the standard kind of protocol that people use Since we're trying to do as proper as possible code code that scales code that can be read by other people We're going to call that self and we're not going to deviate from that I'm not sure i've ever seen anyone deviate from that But you could if you wanted to be a real jerk

Creating object environment

```python
import pygame
import random
WIDTH = 800
HEIGHT = 600
WHITE = (255, 255, 255)
BLUE = (0, 0, 255)
RED = (255, 0, 0)

game_display = pygame.display.set_mode((WIDTH, HEIGHT))
pygame.display.set_caption("Blob World")
clock = pygame.time.Clock()

class Blob:

    def init(self, color):
        self.x = random.randrange(0, WIDTH)
        self.y = random.randrange(0, HEIGHT)
        self.size = random.randrange(4,8)
        self.color = color

    def move(self):
        self.move_x = random.randrange(-1,2)
        self.move_y = random.randrange(-1,2)
        self.x += self.move_x
        self.y += self.move_y

        if self.x < 0: self.x = 0
        elif self.x > WIDTH: self.x = WIDTH
```

```
            if self.y < 0: self.y = 0
            elif self.y > HEIGHT: self.y = HEIGHT


def draw_environment(blob):
        game_display.fill(WHITE)        # redraw background
        pygame.draw.circle(game_display, blob.color, [blob.x,
blob.y], blob.size)
        pygame.display.update()        # sending the final result
        blob.move()


def main():
        red_blob = Blob(RED)     # create the object
        while True:
                for event in pygame.event.get():
                        if event.type == pygame.QUIT:
                                pygame.quit()
                                quit()
                draw_environment(red_blob)
                clock.tick(60)    # frame numbers for a second
        shouldn't exceed this
                print(red_blob.x, red_blob.y)


if name == 'main':
        main()




C:\Users\USER\Desktop\Intermediate-Tutorials>python
intermediate14.py
run the pygame program at command window
----------------------------------------------------------------
510 284
511 284
512 285
512 286
512 285
511 284
511 283
512 284
513 285
```

```
514  286
514  287
514  287
515  287
514  287
```

The user if they slowed the game down enough right or watched it in slow-mo it's not like the background first is going to go all white and then little objects are going to be updated to the screen. That's not how it's going to work what pygame's going to do is truly in the background it's going to okay it's going to say okay we're filling with white and then it says okay. Maybe we're going to draw an object which we will so maybe we've got a blob here. It's going to draw a blob there and then when it's all said and done it's going to say okay. This is the final final result that we actually want to be the new frame and then it sends it to the screen that time for real.

15 Many objects

```python
import pygame
import random
STARTING_BLUE_BLOBS = 10
STARTING_RED_BLOBS = 3
WIDTH = 800
HEIGHT = 600
WHITE = (255, 255, 255)
BLUE = (0, 0, 255)
RED = (255, 0, 0)

game_display = pygame.display.set_mode((WIDTH, HEIGHT))
pygame.display.set_caption("Blob World")
clock = pygame.time.Clock()

class Blob:
    def __init__(self, color):
        self.x = random.randrange(0, WIDTH)
        self.y = random.randrange(0, HEIGHT)
        self.size = random.randrange(4,8)
        self.color = color

    def move(self):
        self.move_x = random.randrange(-1,2)
        self.move_y = random.randrange(-1,2)
        self.x += self.move_x
        self.y += self.move_y

        if self.x < 0: self.x = 0
```

```python
                    elif self.x > WIDTH: self.x = WIDTH
                    if self.y < 0: self.y = 0
                    elif self.y > HEIGHT: self.y = HEIGHT


def draw_environment(blob_list):
        game_display.fill(WHITE)


        for blob_dict in blob_list:
                for blob_id in blob_dict:
                        blob = blob_    dict[blob_id]        #able to
                manage the index of blob
                        pygame.draw.circle(game_display, blob.color,
                [blob.x, blob.y], blob.size)
                        blob.move()
        pygame.display.update()


def main():
        blue_blobs = dict(enumerate([Blob(BLUE) for i in
range(STARTING_BLUE_BLOBS)]))        # gives id for each blob
        red_blobs = dict(enumerate([Blob(RED) for i in
range(STARTING_RED_BLOBS)]))  # when two blobs corride
each other
        print(blue_blobs)        # index, blob objects
        while True:
                for event in pygame.event.get():
                        if event.type == pygame.QUIT:
                                pygame.quit()
                                quit()
                draw_environment([blue_blobs,red_blobs])
                clock.tick(60)
                # print(red_blob.x, red_blob.y)


if __name__ == '__main__':
        main()



*run the pygame program at command window*
C:\Users\USER\Desktop\Intermediate-Tutorials>python
intermediate15.py
```

```
----------------------------------------------------------------------------
{0: <__main__.Blob object at 0x000002D182166BE0>, 1:
<__main__.Blob object at 0x000002D182166780>, 2: <__main__.Blob
object at 0x000002D183BCFC50>, 3: <__main__.Blob object at
0x000002D183BCFF60>, 4: <__main__.Blob object at
0x000002D183BCFF98>, 5: <__main__.Blob object at
0x000002D183BD4A20>, 6: <__main__.Blob object at
0x000002D184BD05F8>, 7: <__main__.Blob object at
0x000002D184BD7828>, 8: <__main__.Blob object at
0x000002D184BF8DD8>, 9: <__main__.Blob object at
0x000002D184BFFC50>}
```

Why do we need an id like well for example we're gonna create red blobs here in a moment and red blobs need or we're gonna just say that when a blue blob collides with a red blob that's a bad thing and maybe the red blob kills the blue blob. We need to know which blue blob is that. So if it's just a without dict and enumerate if it's just this if it's just a list of blob objects we don't know which objects that really it like. We have no way of like being like okay that okay we know that object. Now let's delete that out. We it's really difficult to do that. There's one thing we might do is we could have like some sort of attribute in the blob that says like is alive or something like that. So i mean there are things that we could do to kind of handle for this. But i think it's probably a wise idea to give it the blobs some sort of id. Now we know the blobs' id if something happens to that blob where you can save that some somewhere. So we give that blob an id.

16 OOP modularity

```python
import random
class Blob:
    def __init__(self, color, x_boundary, y_boundary,
size_range=(4,8), movement_range=(-7,7)):
        self.size = random.randrange(size_range[0],
    size_range[1])
        self.color = color
        self.x_boundary = x_boundary
        self.y_boundary = y_boundary
        self.x = random.randrange(0, self.x_boundary)
        self.y = random.randrange(0, self.y_boundary)
        self.movement_range = movement_range

    def move(self):
        self.move_x =
    random.randrange(self.movement_range[0],
    self.movement_range[1])
        self.move_y =
    random.randrange(self.movement_range[0],
    self.movement_range[1])
        self.x += self.move_x
        self.y += self.move_y

    def check_bounds(self):
        if self.x < 0: self.x = 0
        elif self.x > self.x_boundary: self.x =
    self.x_boundary
        if self.y < 0: self.y = 0
        elif self.y > self.y_boundary: self.y =
    self.y_boundary
```

I'm gonna do my best to convince you that you probably need to be doing something completely different before You even write your class entirely but we'll get there at some point But at least for your simple class is probably the big takeaway Here is that you'll want to think about you don't necessarily have to I'm not a huge proponent of taking your programs or whatever and just turning them into these huge libraries. But I am a big fan of making sure your code can be modular if and when possible And it's too easy when you write it all in line with your main whatever your main execution is It can be too easy to do it all together and wind up using things like your constants and stuffs like that and not realizing that's not going to be acceptable for either you to use the code later on or for anyone else to use your code

17 OOP Inheritance

```python
class BlueBlob(Blob):    # a child class of Blob
    def __init__(self, color, x_boundary, y_boundary):
            super().__init__(color, x_boundary, y_boundary)
    #what super enables? multiple inheritance
            self.color = BLUE

    def move_fast(self):    #create a new mothod
            self.x += random.randrange(-1, 2)
            self.y += random.randrange(-1, 2)

def main():
    blue_blobs = dict(enumerate([BlueBlob(BLUE, WIDTH, HEIGHT)
for i in range(STARTING_BLUE_BLOBS)]))
```

how could we have an init method for both classes?(parent and child) Well that's where super comes into play. And so instead what we can do is we can say something like this We can say super() and then dot underscore underscore init so we're just basically we're running the init method for the super class whatever that super class might be and we're gonna say color x_boundary and y_boundary and then of course because we're doing that this is all now this is all contained within our init method we're using these parameters here So we need to pass them as well and a space there And for now I'm just gonna do well we can leave blue there that should be fine So now everything's gonna be blue though So where we say red blobs it it's going to actually change them to blue So let's go ahead and run that And now sure enough all we have are blue blobs ... So the only other thing that people might be uncomfortable with is the use of super here It's you could get away with doing something like we could say here We could say Blob dot init and then we have to pass the instance So we would say self because like in that we use sup when your're using super you don't have to pass self but in this case you do right We're actually missing one positional argument because this was being passed itself But if we pass self here this will work and sure enough it works but now it's a form of hard coding and in this case it's not a big deal But at some point you're gonna come across a time when you want to engage in what's called multiple inheritance and this is going to cause a whole lot of problems So instead we use super init and we don't have the self there

파이썬 프로그래밍 **코딩영어**

18 Decorators

```
'''
@app.route('/contact/')
def contact():
      return render_template("contact.html")
'''
from functools import wraps    #OOP programming application

def add_wrapping_with_style(style):
      def add_wrapping(item):
            @wraps(item)     #won't allow item to get the
      control newly
            def wrapped_item():
                  return 'a {} wrapped up box of
            {}'.format(style,str(item()))
            return wrapped_item
      return add_wrapping
@add_wrapping_with_style('horribly')
@add_wrapping_with_style('beautifully')
def new_gpu():
      return 'a new Tesla P100 GPU'
print(new_gpu())
print(new_gpu.__name__)          #shows the original function
name still on control

'''
from functools import wraps    #OOP programming application
def add_wrapping(item):
      @wraps(item)        #won't allow item to get the control
newly
```

```python
        def wrapped_item():
                return 'a wrapped up box of {}'.format(str(item()))
        return wrapped_item


@add_wrapping
def new_bicycle():
        return 'a new bicycle'


print(new_bicycle())
print(new_bicycle.__name__)   #shows the original function
name still on control
'''
```

Now since you guys are sending it to me for Christmas maybe you want to wrap the gpu So you might have a new function and we'll say define add wrapping When you wrap something you're wrapping right you're wrapping something So you're gonna pass whatever the item is that you want to wrap into this wrapping function this will be our decorator function And now we're going to say we're gonna define wrapped underscore item and what this is gonna do is return a wrapped up box of something and then will do dot format string version of whatever the item is So we return that and then now at the that for the actual add wrapping function we're gonna return wrapped item So now what we can do is at new gpu we can wrap it So we can say boom add wrapping and that will decorate our wrapping paper to our new Tesla P100 gpu So we can now run literally new gpu nothing changes We've just added that wrapping with the decorator

19 Operator overloading

```python
class BlueBlob(Blob):
    def __init__(self, x_boundary, y_boundary):
        Blob.__init__(self, (0, 0, 255), x_boundary,
        y_boundary)
    def __add__(self, other_blob):      # define + add dunder
method
        if other_blob.color == (255, 0, 0):     # when meets
    red blob,
            self.size -= other_blob.size       # subtract me
        by red's size
            other_blob.size -= self.size       # again,
        subtract red by my size
        elif other_blob.color == (0, 255, 0):   # when meets
        green blob,
            self.size += other_blob.size       # add me by
        green's size
            other_blob.size = 0   # and make the green
        disappear
            elif other_blob.color == (0, 0, 255):   # when
        meets blue
                pass      # don't touch anything
            else:
                raise Exception('Tried to combine one
            or multiple blobs of unsupported colors.')

def main():
    blue_blobs = dict(enumerate([BlueBlob(WIDTH,HEIGHT) for
i in range(STARTING_BLUE_BLOBS)]))
```

```
    red_blobs = dict(enumerate([RedBlob(WIDTH,HEIGHT) for i
in range(STARTING_RED_BLOBS)]))
    green_blobs = dict(enumerate([GreenBlob(WIDTH,HEIGHT)
 for i in range(STARTING_GREEN_BLOBS)]))
    # print(red_blobs)
    print('Blue blob size:{} red size:
{}'.format(blue_blobs[0].size, red_blobs[0].size))
    blue_blobs[0] + red_blobs[0]
    print('Blue blob size:{} red size:
{}'.format(blue_blobs[0].size, red_blobs[0].size))
```

Now i want to do is begin adding interaction between these blobs jects Anyway what i'd like to be able to do is say okay when a blue and a red blob come into contact wouldn't it be nice if we could just say Let's say you've got a blue blob that's a blue blob object variable name for now and then you've got a red blob object Wouldn't it be cool if we could just say like plus Right because this was really happening they're combing the they're banging into each other We want to be able to use plus okay ... Today we're just gonna do the plus sign and what's cool is as you'll see the way that we do it is it's it'll be unlike any other method It's just it's just it's cool So anyways let's get started So to do it it's a magic method a special method It's dunder add So define dunder add as always We have to pass self But when you had an add operation you're adding you know you've got one thing plus something else it'll be the second parameter or whatever that is and that in our case should be another blob right You're gonna add blobs together in theory It could be something else but for now let's just say it's a blob great So now basically it could be any of a handful of blobs right It could be a red blob a green blob or a blue blob So we need to handle for each of those ... So really if red blob is larger than the blue blob it's lights out for the blue blob and he's not really gonna do any damage to the red blob So keep that in mind And in fact it might but it could even add to the size

⑳ Collision detection

```python
def is_touching(b1, b2):                   # distance of two blobs' x, y
positions comparing to those two radius' sum
    return np.linalg.norm(np.array([b1.x, b1.y])-np.array([b2.x,
b2.y])) < (b1.size + b2.size)


def handle_collisions(blob_list):
    blues, reds, greens = blob_list           # seperate each blob's
dictionary
    for blue_id, blue_blob, in blues.copy().items():  # copy
the item for not modify purpose only
        for other_blobs in blues, reds, greens:
            for other_blob_id, other_blob in
other_blobs.copy().items():
                if blue_blob == other_blob:
                    pass
                else:
                    if is_touching(blue_blob, other_blob):
                        blue_blob + other_blob   # calls +
            dunder add function
                        if other_blob.size <= 0:
                            del other_blobs[other_blob_id]
                        if blue_blob.size <= 0:
                            del blues[blue_id]
    return blues, reds, greens    # what specifically is
returned?


def draw_environment(blob_list):
    blues, reds, greens = handle_collisions(blob_list)
```

```
        return blues, reds, greens    # what specifically is
returned?

def main():
            blue_blobs,red_blobs,green_blobs =
        draw_environment([blue_blobs,red_blobs,green_blobs])
            clock.tick(60)
```

We're gonna import numpy as np and then we're going to come on down and above draw environment We're gonna add a new function or say define is touching and it's gonna take two parameters b1, b2 for blob 1 and blob 2 and then we're just gonna ask if np dot linal for linear algebra dot norm for the norm if that of basically and the word i say np dot array of b1 x b1 y so these are the locations of that blob and again this could be on an infinite dimensional plane So you have three dimensions 15 dimensions or in our case just simple two dimensions so it's Euclidean distance But you could go further if you wanted if you had 3d blobs for example this would still work Let's see before i get myself lost you want to take that it's the norm and when you calculate the norm it'll be that minus basically the same thing only b2 okay If that is less than b1 dot size plus b2 dot size then we'll put spaces around plus because we're good we're PEP 8ers If that's the case you know we want to return true otherwise we would return false ... So that's how we know if they're touching

21 Special methods, OOP, iteration

```python
x = range(5)      # 'range' generator has no attribute
'__next__', but has __iter__
##
##x = (i for i in range(5))   # 'range' generate expression
##
##x.__next__()    # but this one works, which means has
attribute '__next__'
##x.__next__()
##
for i in x:       # this is just an iterable, which enables selection
of data
        print(i)
##
##
## # when class object called, python just automatically gives
all those methods for you to use.
##
##class range_examp:
##
##    def __init__(self, end, step=1):
##            self.current = 0
##            self.end = end
##            self.step = step
##
##    def __iter__(self):
##            return self
##
##    def __next__(self):
```

```
##            if self.current >= self.end:
##                raise StopIteration()
##        else:
##                return_val = self.current
##                self.current += self.step
##                return return_val
##
##x = range_examp(5)
##
##x.__next__()
##next(x)
##
##for i in x:
##    print(i)
##
####for i in range_examp(5):
####        print(i)
##
##
## # generator object alone when called gives method '__iter__',
'__next__' also
##
##def range_gen(end):
##    current = 0
##    while current < end:
##        yield current
##        current += 1
##
##x = range_gen(5)
##
##x.__next__()
##
##for i in x:
##    print(i)
##
####for i in range_gen(5):
####        print(i)
####
####
```

```
####  let's see what happens on system console
####
####dir(range_gen)        # no __iter__, no __next__
####dir(range_gen(5))    # __iter__ and __next__
####
####
####  let's see with simple range()
####
####dir(range)              # __iter__ but no __next__
####dir(range(5))           # __iter__ but no __next__
####dir((i for i in range(5)))      # __iter__ and __next__
```

Let's say for i in x we're just gonna iterate that We'll print i 0 1 2 3 4 just what we expected Now what you might not know is you can actually you can Rather than using a for loop you can move the iterator on your own manually explicitly and the way that you can do that is with next So we can actually say next x next x And what we're doing there is we're like we're literally moving this iterator The iterator you can think of it like a selector or something where it just kind of moves along one at a time especially as you're doing like a for loop It's just gonna move that selector one at a time And so what we can do save it and run that and you'll see now as we've already moved the selector twice and then we iterate through it So the way that it works An iterator as it iterates over an iterable it's gonna just keep going and just keep doing this like the next next next next until it reaches a stop iteration ... Maybe it's a surprise though that dunder next is a valid method of x it's there it exists x as an object Everything in Python is an object Python is an object oriented language So we can print actually don't even need to print We need to say dir x because i'm in the shell here Let me say holy moley We've got a lot of attributes and little dunders that we didn't even know about right

22 Logging

```python
import logging
'''

DEBUG Detailed information, typically of interest only when diagnosing problems.
INFO Confirmation that things are working as expected.
WARNING An indication that something unexpected happened, or indicative of some
problem in the near future (e.g. 'disk space low'). The software is still working as
expected.
ERROR Due to a more serious problem, the software has not been able to perform
some function.
CRITICAL A serious error, indicating that the program itself may be unable to continue
running.
'''
logging.basicConfig(filename='logfile.log', level=logging.INFO)
STARTING_BLUE_BLOBS = 15
STARTING_RED_BLOBS = 7
STARTING_GREEN_BLOBS = 10


class BlueBlob(Blob):
    def __init__(self, x_boundary, y_boundary):
        Blob.__init__(self, (0, 0, 255), x_boundary, y_boundary)
    def __add__(self, other_blob):
        logging.info('Blob add op {} + {}'.format(str(self.color),
    str(other_blob.color)))
        if other_blob.color == (255, 0, 0):
            self.size -= other_blob.size
            other_blob.size -= self.size
        elif other_blob.color == (0, 255, 0):
            self.size += other_blob.size
```

파이썬 프로그래밍 **코딩영어**

```python
                other_blob.size = 0
            elif other_blob.color == (0, 0, 255):
                pass
            else:
                raise Exception('Tried to combine one or multiple
                blobs of unsupported colors.')

def handle_collisions(blob_list):
    blues, reds, greens = blob_list        # seperate each blob's
dictionary
    for blue_id, blue_blob, in blues.copy().items():  # copy
the item except modifing purpose only
        for other_blobs in blues, reds, greens:
            for other_blob_id, other_blob in
other_blobs.copy().items():
                logging.debug('Checking if blobs are touching {} +
    {}'.format(str(blue_blob.color), str(other_blob.color)))
                if blue_blob == other_blob:
                    pass
                else:
                    if is_touching(blue_blob, other_blob):
                        blue_blob + other_blob        # calls +
                    dunder add function
                        if other_blob.size <= 0:
                            del other_blobs[other_blob_id]
                        if blue_blob.size <= 0:
                            del blues[blue_id]
    return blues, reds, greens    # what specifically is
returned?

def main():
    while True:
        try:
            for event in pygame.event.get():
                if event.type == pygame.QUIT:
                    pygame.quit()
                    quit()
        except Exception as e:
            logging.critical(str(e))
```

```
        pygame.quit()
        quit()
        break

    blue_blobs,red_blobs,green_blobs =
draw_environment([blue_blobs,red_blobs,green_blobs])
        clock.tick(60)

if __name__ == '__main__':
    main()
```

What you can do with logging is you can set certain levels so for example Let's go ahead an import logging and then let's set up and configure it So we can do logging dot basic config camel case there level equals logging dot and we'll say info for now So any log information that we say is debug level under this configuration won't actually log I mean the codes there but it's not gonna log because we're setting the logging level to info So everything info and above will log But the debug lay level stuff just isn't gonna log either It's not going to come to our console and or go to our file so But we can change that So like let's say for some reason something went really awry and we don't know what's up and maybe we even had it set toe just warning and then we checked a log file and sure enough Oh we've got a log of warnings in here but we're not seeing exactly what's wrong We might later decide ok let's set it to debug Run everything again and see what's happening and so It's just a really quick way to change one thing and get a whole lot more information from your program as apposed to the typical you know

23 Error handling

```python
import sys
import logging

def error_handling():
    return '{}. {}, line: {}'.format(sys.exc_info()[0],
                                     sys.exc_info()[1],
                                     sys.exc_info()[2].tb_lineno)
try:
    a + b
except Exception as e:
    logging.error(error_handling())

'''

    print(sys.exc_info()[0])
    print(sys.exc_info()[1])
    print(sys.exc_info()[2].tb_lineno)
    print(sys.exc_info())
    print(str(e))
a + b
'''
```

So first we're going to do is we're going to import sys Now what sys is gonna let us do is actually access the trace back itself the actual exception error and then we can and then we can start returning information from that error So rather than print string e we can do something like this like Let's print sys dot exc for exception info and let's just do that for now Save and run that and as you can see it's actually a tuple of some information for us We've got what kind of error was it and then we actually literally get the error And then we get this trace back object blah blah The trace back object is the actual information of like the line number and other bits of information for us Let's close that and instead what we're going to do is we're gonna slice this up Now interestingly enough i read from the internet's that in exception it's unwise to save the slices to variables So for example you might wanted well first let's just do this Let me just print it out So well let's just print the slices So zero we'll do it will print that And now i'm going to paste this three times or two times rather one and two So the zeroth was the error This was the name error And then this would be like that trace back information And we can say tb underscore line number lineno for line number Let's save and run that okay You get name err name a is not defined line four

24 __str__ and __repr__

```python
import random

class Blob:
    def init(self, color, x_boundary, y_boundary,
size_range=(4,8), movement_range=(-7,7)):
        self.size = random.randrange(size_range[0],
    size_range[1])
        self.color = color
        self.x_boundary = x_boundary
        self.y_boundary = y_boundary
        self.x = random.randrange(0, self.x_boundary)
        self.y = random.randrange(0, self.y_boundary)
        self.movement_range = movement_range
def repr(self):
    return 'Blob({}, {}, ({}, {}))'.format(self.color,
                                            self.size,
                                            self.x,
                                            self.y)
def str(self):
    return "Color: {} blobject of size {}. Located at
{},{}".format(self.color,
        self.size,
        self.x,
        self.y)

class BlueBlob(Blob):
    def __init__(self, x_boundary, y_boundary):
        Blob.__init__(self, (0, 0, 255), x_boundary,
    y_boundary)
```

```python
    def __add__(self, other_blob):
        logging.info('Blob add op {} + {}'.format(str(self),
str(other_blob)))
        if other_blob.color == (255, 0, 0):
            self.size -= other_blob.size
            other_blob.size -= self.size
        elif other_blob.color == (0, 255, 0):
            self.size += other_blob.size
            other_blob.size = 0
        elif other_blob.color == (0, 0, 255):
            pass
        else:
            raise Exception('Tried to combine one or
multiple blobs of unsupported colors.')

if name == 'main':
    blue_blobs = dict(enumerate([BlueBlob(WIDTH,HEIGHT) for
i in range(STARTING_BLUE_BLOBS)]))
    red_blobs = dict(enumerate([RedBlob(WIDTH,HEIGHT) for i
in range(STARTING_RED_BLOBS)]))
    green_blobs = dict(enumerate([GreenBlob(WIDTH,HEIGHT)
for i in range(STARTING_GREEN_BLOBS)]))
    pygame.quit()

#main()
```

Now what i'm going to go ahead and do is head on over to the actual blob dot py So this is the that what we're actually importing this is our blob class the base class anyways They are the parent class We are modifying that up here with the blue blobs and the red blobs and the green blob But we don't have to give each of these their own repr method We actually just need we could just do it in this parent class here So what i'll do is just come down here and now i'm going to go ahead and do a dunder repr and we just need to pass self we do need the other dunder though and now we're gonna do is just obviously it just returns a string right And like we were saying the repr method's really more kind of for debugging purposes It should be as condensed as possible We're not really it's not really meant to be output to a console in production use It's just really for debugging ... So now we have repr method Let's save that let's pop on over to blob world Looks good And now let's print blue blobs zero and now at least we have something a little more useful We've got the color again this is an RGB the size and then the x y coordinates location

25 *args and **kwargs

```python
site_title = 'My Blog'
def blog_posts(title, *args, **kwargs):
    print(title)
    for arg in args:
        print(arg)
    for p_title, post in kwargs.items():
        print(p_title, post)

blog_posts(site_title,
        '1', '2', '3',
        blog_1 = 'I am so awesome.',
        blog_2 = 'Cars are cool.',
        blog_3 = 'Aww look at my cat!!')
```

So let's say you've got a website we're gonna just kind of already use really simple code here I'm not going to implement this necessarily into the blob class that we've been working on in this series um So let's just take like a really simple example Let's say you've got a blog and you've got blog number one of course It's like I am so awesome there's something like that most likely is what you're talking about and then blog two ... blog three ... So let's start with define blog posts and if you wanted a function that was gonna take all your blog posts You might just use args like so and then what we could say is for post in args Let's just print the post So now we can come over here and we can say a blog posts and let's say for now you just started your blog you just have blog one I know we wrote blog two and three already but right now we just want to host blog number one Maybe we want to go back and edit the cars and cat one So we've saved and run that and what we get is just that one blog I am so awesome Now later on you just say yeah i'm ready to publish the other blog so blog two blog three Notice that we're just throwing these in just like regular parameters here like we're just stuffing them on in there we just have the args like this right So let's run it again and boom It works it args lets you just throw in an unlimited number of arguments crazy

(26) Asyncio

```python
import asyncio
# docs.python.org/3.6/library/asyncio-eventloop.html

async def find_divisibles(inrange, div_by):
    print("finding nums in range {} divisible by
{}".format(inrange, div_by))
    located = []
    for i in range(inrange):
        if i % div_by == 0:
            located.append(i)
        if i % 500000 == 0:
            await asyncio.sleep(0.0001)

    print("Done w/ nums in range {} divisible by
{}".format(inrange, div_by))
    return located
# Next, let's add a main() function, which will serve as our main
block of code that executes these functions:
async def main():         # usual mistake2 - without async, you gonna
get syntaxError
    divs1 = loop.create_task(find_divisibles(508000, 34113))
    divs2 = loop.create_task(find_divisibles(100052, 3210))
    divs3 = loop.create_task(find_divisibles(500, 3))
    await asyncio.wait([divs1,divs2,divs3])  # usual
mistake1 - without await, task destroyed and is pending
    return divs1, divs2, divs3

# Finally, let's just run the main function:
```

```python
if __name__ == '__main__':
    try:
        loop = asyncio.get_event_loop() #initialize loop for
us
        loop.set_debug(1)
        d1, d2, d3 = loop.run_until_complete(main())
        print(d1.result())
    except Exception as e:
        pass
    finally:
        loop.close()
```

We're just running this task so in this case this is a bulk task This isn't really a request to a server while we wait for a response and then during that wait for a response we could do something else So instead what i'm gonna do is we're just gonna add a little tiny bit of wait basically right here So in this case we're just as we iterate through that range we're asking is it divisible by what are the div by is If it is, we're gonna append it to located But the other we're gonna have one more thing We're gonna say if i modulo and then in this case we can use anything it depends on really what this big task is Like you would probably want to logically do this you could make it a number as large as a hundred thousand or larger than a hundred thousand and then this would never get hit And i'll show you if that's not if you've not following my logic yet that's okay So let me actually just write it out So let's say 50,000 So i is divisible by 50,000 then what we're gonna do is just momentarily suspend this this co-routine

쉽게 더 쉽게 ~ 배우는 코딩영어

팔하나
Palhana
8-1

난 코딩을 영어로 바로 배운다

- 코딩을 영어 스피치를 들으면서 따라하는 실습은 영어실력이 대단하지 않음 어렵다고들 생각합니다

- 누구든 쉽게 자기 주도로 학습할 수 있게, 앞서 LC훈련을 통해 원본 비디오를 요점 정리 해드립니다

- 원본 비디오 15-20분 에서 가장 잘 안 들리는 1-2분을 집중해서 파고들어 봅니다. 그럼, 나머지 부분은 절로 쉽게 따라할 수 있게 된답니다.

- 6개월이면, 귀가 뻥~ 뚫려서 코딩과 영어에서 자유로워 집니다

- 이 후로는 원하는 주제의 비디오를 선택해서 온전하게 자기 주도로 학습이 가능해집니다

- 초5-고1 대상인 쉽게 더 쉽게 ~ 배우는 코딩영어는 월 수강료가 15만원

PART III

Django web development:
Tutorial model

처음 코딩할 때 영어 speech를 들으면서 실습하는 습관을 길들이는 것은 매우 중요합니다! 대한민국 모든 청소년들이 너도 나도 코딩영어로 무장해 담대하게 세상에 나아가게 해드리는 것이 저희 목표입니다. 저희가 개발한 이 자기주도학습법이 왜 우수할까요?

1. 코딩은 영어로 만든 용어요, 문법이라 영어로 들었을 때 가장 쉽게 이해가 가게 되어 있다.

2. 실습을 해서 결과가 맞게 나오면 영어가 들렸다는 얘기니깐, 혼자서도 학습이 절로 된다.

3. 정 이해가 안 되고 실습 결과가 계속 다르게 나오면, 그땐 코딩영어의 도움을 받으면 된다.

유튜브에서 강의 제목과 'sentdex'로 검색하심 Harrison Kinsley의 원본 비디오가 나옵니다. LC training(6:20). 괄호 안의 숫자는 거기 비디오가 시작되는 지점을 말합니다.

1 Send/Recv

이제부턴 응용 모듈 개발에 들어갑니다.

세계에서 제일 머리 좋다는 한국, 일본 사람들이 왜 코딩에서만큼은 뒤처지고 있을까요? 처음 배울 때 습관이 중요한데, 굳이 영어로 된 코딩을 자기네 말로 바꾸어서 배우는 학습법의 문제라는 게 제 주장입니다! 서양사람들은 다들 이렇게 코딩을 배운답니다. 어떻게? 귀로 화자의 speech를 들으면서 눈으로 보고 실습을 따라 합니다. 솔직히 이보다 더 효과적인 코딩 학습법은 아직까지 나온게 없습니다.

sockets server/client에서 send/receive 기능을 간단히 구현합니다.

```python
import socket
# create the socket
# AF_INET == ipv4
# SOCK_STREAM == TCP
s = socket.socket(socket.AF_INET, socket.SOCK_STREAM)
s.bind((socket.gethostname(), 1234))
s.listen(5)                # queue of five

while True:
    # now our endpoint knows about the OTHER endpoint.
    clientsocket, address = s.accept()
    print(f"Connection from {address} has been established!")
    clientsocket.send(bytes("Welcome to the server!","utf-
8"))
    clientsocket.close()
```

```
import socket
s = socket.socket(socket.AF_INET, socket.SOCK_STREAM)
s.connect((socket.gethostname(), 1234))

full_msg = ''
while True:
    msg = s.recv(8 )          # 8 bytes long
    if len(msg) <= 0:
        break
    full_msg += msg.decode("utf-8")
print(full_msg)
```

Now what we want to do is define our socket object So s equals socket dot socket and the socket family type is AF_INET and then the actual type of socket is going to be socket dot SOCK_STREAM Now INET corresponds to IPV4 and SOCK_STREAM corresponds to TCP so this will be a streaming socket ... Now what we want to do is bind to that socket So s dot bind and we want to bind it to a tuple based on sometimes this will be different but anyway the tuple will be in this case because of the type of socket an IP and a port Now this is our server so we're actually just gonna host the server on the same machine that we have the code So we're gonna bind to socket dot get host-name so whatever the host name is basically localhost and then the port we're gonna go with one two three four ... also let's talk real briefly what even is a socket? So a socket is just the endpoint Generally you're gonna have like two endpoints right to have a communication So that's just the end point that receives data So with a socket you send in you receive data So the socket itself is not the communication it's just the end point that like receives that communication on that end point sits at an IP and a port So we will s dot bind that socket

2 Buffering

socket에서 buffer size를 결정하는 건 상당히 까다로운 일입니다. 적어도 안 되고 너무 많아도 안 됩니다. 하지만 과연 얼마나 긴 사이즈의 메시지가 날아올지 사전에 미리 예측하기란 어렵기만 합니다. 그래서 나온 방식이 header를 만들어 줘서 메시지 앞에다 위치케 해서 내보내는 해결책입니다. 받게 되면 그 헤더 사이즈만 받아들이는 겁니다. 헤더 사이즈는 fixed length로 미리 정해 주는 것이 가능한 것이 헤더 n 자리에는 10의 n승 사이즈만큼의 characters를 내 보낼 수 있기 때문에 사이즈를 미리 여유 있게 잡아 놓을 수 있습니다. 어떻게 한다고요? 실습을 통해서 익히도록 하십시다.

```
server:
import socket
import time
HEADERSIZE = 10
while True:
    msg = "Welcome to the server!"
    msg = f"{len(msg):<{HEADERSIZE}}" + msg
    clientsocket.send(bytes(msg,"utf-8"))
    while True:
        time.sleep(3)
        msg = f"The time is {time.time()}"
        msg = f"{len(msg):<{HEADERSIZE}}" + msg
        clientsocket.send(bytes(msg,"utf-8"))


client:
import socket
HEADERSIZE = 10
while True:
```

```python
full_msg = ''
new_msg = True
while True:
    msg = s.recv(16)
    if new_msg:
        print("new msg len:",msg[:HEADERSIZE])
        msglen = int(msg[:HEADERSIZE])
        new_msg = False
    full_msg += msg.decode("utf-8")
```

So you can't just say len message because that might be you know if it's under 100 it could be two characters one character If it's greater than 100 be three characters We need it to be a fixed length so how do we do that So the way we're going to do that First you have to kind of decide well what is like the longest message we could ever receive okay I'm gonna go with 10 so 10 would be that's 1 comma so it's 4 7 10 so if you're thinking you're gonna get a message longer than 1 billion characters do something even bigger okay But for now i'm gonna go with 10 So what we're gonna say is print and then this will be f so we're gonna use the f string here and then we're gonna say len message and then and this will be colon less than and then whatever that header length is In this case we're gonna say it's 10 So now we'll print that out and you see it says 22 but what you don't see is the extra characters But if i highlight it you can see it It's a fixed length it's 10 characters The next thing we could do is we could actually append to it the original message So we'll do that and now you can see here it precedes the message

3 Send/Recv objects

Python에선 pickle이라는 아주 편리한 object file 송수신 기능이 있습니다. 실습에선 간단한 dictionary를 하나 만들어서 그 object를 sockets 간에 주고받아 봅니다.

```
server:
import socket
import pickle
HEADERSIZE = 10
s = socket.socket(socket.AF_INET, socket.SOCK_STREAM)
s.bind((socket.gethostname(), 1236))
s.listen(5)
while True:
        clientsocket, address = s.accept()
        print(f"Connection from {address} has been established.")
        d = {1: "hey", 2: "there"}
        msg = pickle.dumps(d)
        msg = bytes(f'{len(msg):<{HEADERSIZE}}', "utf-8") + msg
        clientsocket.send(msg)


client:
import socket
import pickle
HEADERSIZE = 10
s = socket.socket(socket.AF_INET, socket.SOCK_STREAM)
s.connect((socket.gethostname(), 1236))
while True:
        full_msg = b''
        new_msg = True
```

```
    while True:
        msg = s.recv(16)

        if len(full_msg)-HEADERSIZE == msglen:
            print("full msg recvd")
            print(full_msg[HEADERSIZE:])
            d = pickle.loads(full_msg[HEADERSIZE:])
            print(d)
            new_msg = True
            full_msg = b""
print(full_msg)
```

So that's the thing that we want a pickle so how do we do that? Well we're gonna just say message the message we want to receive later is gonna be pickle dot dumps d and we can just print message real quickly to see okay Here's what we've got basically we do have the string data that we can see here Um we also i don't see the number but it's probably there somewhere anyway and then we've got some gobbledygook that is the information that is contained within the actual structuring of what a dictionary is and how we can interact with it and all that cool So now we want to send this information so let's go ahead and do that So i'm gonna cut that come over here come down here or fix that okay Get rid of this loop we don't we're not gonna loop anymore And the message now let me just get rid of the first one paste this on in So now our message is that pickle dump but we also we still want to use that header again because the thing we pickle might very easily exceed our buffer size so we need to be able to handle for that

④ Chat server

```python
# Handles message receiving
def receive_message(client_socket):
    try:
        message_header =
client_socket.recv(HEADER_LENGTH)
        if not len(message_header):
            return False
        message_length = int(message_header.decode('utf-
8').strip())
        return {'header': message_header, 'data':
client_socket.recv(message_length)}
    except:
        return False


while True:
    read_sockets, _, exception_sockets =
select.select(sockets_list, [], sockets_list)
    # Iterate over notified sockets
    for notified_socket in read_sockets:
        # If notified socket is a server socket - new
connection, accept it
        if notified_socket == server_socket:
            client_socket, client_address =
server_socket.accept()
            user = receive_message(client_socket)
            if user is False:
                continue
            sockets_list.append(client_socket)
```

파이썬 프로그래밍 **코딩영어**

```python
                clients[client_socket] = user
                print('Accepted new connection from {}:{},
        username: {}'.format(*client_address,
        user['data'].decode('utf-8')))
    # Else existing socket is sending a message
    else:

        message = receive_message(notified_socket)
        if message is False:
            print('Closed connection from:
        {}'.format(clients[notified_socket]['data'].decode('u
        tf-8')))
            sockets_list.remove(notified_socket)
            del clients[notified_socket]
            continue
        # Get user by notified socket, so we will know who
    sent the message
        user = clients[notified_socket]
        print(f"Received message from
    {user['data'].decode('utf-8')}:
    {message['data'].decode('utf-8')}")
        # Iterate over connected clients and broadcast
    message
        for client_socket in clients:
            # But don't send it to sender
            if client_socket != notified_socket:
                client_socket.send(user['header'] +
            user['data'] + message['header'] +
            message['data'])
    # It's not really necessary to have this, but will handle
some socket exceptions just in case
    for notified_socket in exception_sockets:
        sockets_list.remove(notified_socket)
        del clients[notified_socket]
```

So now we need to do is basically the main thing that the server is going to do and that is simply receive messages So we're going to create some space and let's say define receive underscore message and the parameter here will be from any client socket Now we want to do is try and then except i'm gonna just write pass here we'll fill that in in a moment So what we want to attempt to do is first of all we want to receive the message header and that's going to be a client socket dot receive and then we want to receive whatever the header length is and that will give us the header And then if not len message header so basically we didn't get a thing So if we didn't get any data the client closed the connection so we just need to handle for this So we're just gonna say return false Otherwise what we wanna say is a message length equals whatever the int value of message header dot decode utf-8 and that's it ... So now we're gonna return a dictionary where the value is so for header we're just gonna say the message header and then we're gonna pass data and data will be client socket dot receive and then whatever the message length is So in this case we're just going to receive exactly however long that is

5) Chat client

```python
# Prepare username and header and send them
username = my_username.encode('utf-8')
username_header =
f"{len(username):<{HEADER_LENGTH}}".encode('utf-8')
client_socket.send(username_header + username)
while True:
    # Wait for user to input a message
    message = input(f'{my_username} > ')
    # If message is not empty - prepare message and header
and send them
    if message:
        message = message.encode('utf-8')
        message_header =
f"{len(message):<{HEADER_LENGTH}}".encode('utf-8')
        client_socket.send(message_header + message)
    try:
        # Now we want to loop over received messages
(there might be more than one) and print them
        while True:
            # Receive our "header" containing username
        length, it's size is defined and constant
            username_header =
client_socket.recv(HEADER_LENGTH)
            # If we received no data, server gracefully
        closed a connection, for example using
        socket.close() or
        socket.shutdown(socket.SHUT_RDWR)
            if not len(username_header):
```

```
                    print('Connection closed by the
            server')
                    sys.exit()
            # Convert header to int value
            username_length =
    int(username_header.decode('utf-8').strip())
            # Receive and decode username
            username =
    client_socket.recv(username_length).decode('utf-8')
            # Now do the same for message (as we
    received username, we received whole message,
    there's no need to check if it has any length)
            message_header =
    client_socket.recv(HEADER_LENGTH)
            message_length =
    int(message_header.decode('utf-8').strip())
            message =
    client_socket.recv(message_length).decode('utf-8')
            # Print message
            print(f'{username} > {message}')
    except IOError as e:
        if e.errno != errno.EAGAIN and e.errno !=
    errno.EWOULDBLOCK:
            print('Reading error: {}'.format(str(e)))
            sys.exit()
        # We just did not receive anything
        continue
    except Exception as e:
        print('Reading error: '.format(str(e)))
        sys.exit()
```

So first of all we're gonna say user name under score header equals client socket dot receive header length and then if not len username header whoops amen if not len username header means we basically didn't get any data for whatever reason we're going to say print connection closed by the server and then we run sys dot exit and import sys okay So other than that we want to convert that that username header to an int So what we're going to say is username underscore length equals the int value of username header dot decode utf-8 and then again like before we'll throw in a strip because normally you'd have to do that but i don't think you do here Ah username length okay so we've got the username length Now what we want to grab knowing that header you know what the length of this message of username alone would be we can actually grab the username here So that's gonna be client socket dot receive username length dot decode utf-8 okay So we've got the username now Oh we need to get next is the message itself So coming down here(Sockets 4 17:54) recall when we send information we're sending this right we're sending the user header followed by the username and the header just contains how long is the username and then in that exact same message here but just right after it we're gonna receive the message header and data and now recall this is coming in a stream So we've accepted this exact amount we've accepted the exact amount that is the header data then the header then the username header data let's call it And then again now at the point of data will be exactly at the header for the actual message itself

1 Introduction

```html
<html>
    <body>
        <script>
            alert("hey why you leaving !!!");
            document.write("hey there");
            console.log("thing here of note");
            console.warn("thing here of note");
            console.error("thing here of note");
        </script>
    </body>
</html>

<html>
    <body>
        <canvas id ="myCanvas" width="200px" hight="200px"
style="border: 1px solid #000"></canvas>
        <script>
            const canvas =
        document.getElementById("myCanvas");
            const context = canvas.getContext("2d");

            context.beginPath();
            context.moveTo(10,10);
            context.lineTo(50,25);
            context.stroke();
        </script>
    </body>
</html>
```

So let's try built in JavaScript MDN right so check this out these are all your built-in objects it's a huge freaking list These are things that are just there all the time So things like math and date stuff and all that they're just there and you can use them So anyways one of the things that's there is alert It is everybody's honestly everybody just love it when you have alerts on your webpage i know alert is maybe my favorite thing to ever run into hey why you leaving So for example here's just a really quick alert let's check it out it's just a like a pop-up notification basically So a lot of times you try to leave a website you might see something like this Ah sometimes it's useful if it's like if you have a website like a blog or you know maybe an email site or something where if you leave you're literally gonna lose a thing that you've been working on So you might have missed clicked or something And so you might have a little pop-up that's like hey are you sure But otherwise you can just throw it at people who are trying to bounce off your site and people will just love it so So anyway alert awesome You can also use javascript to write directly to you like as html So for example we can use document dot write Now this is like a little challenging you see this all the time in an intro tutorials So i guess i feel ok throwing it in But document is an object write is a method and these parentheses here encase parameters So you could just point to the method but you can actually run the method with parentheses So you sometimes you might see methods that are just empty parentheses because there's no need for parameters In this case it does take a parameter and it's what you actually want to write

2) Functions

```html
<html>
    <body>
        <canvas id ="myCanvas" width="200px" hight="200px"
    style="border: 1px solid #000"></canvas>
        <script>
            const canvas =
        document.getElementById("myCanvas");
            const context = canvas.getContext("2d");

            function blob(x, y, size, color){
                context.beginPath();
                context.arc(x,y,size,0,2*Math.PI);
                context.fillstyle = color;
                context.fill();
                context.stroke();
            }
            blob(25, 100, 20, "green");
            blob(75, 25, 20, "red");
            blob(50, 65, 20, "blue");
        </script>
    </body>
</html>
```

Now what if what if we wanted to have multiple blobs like this How would we actually do that And the way that we would wind up doing that you know you might think Well i'll just haha i'll just copy and paste hey I'm an expert computer person and you you could do that But you probably don't want to do that right like we definitely just copy and paste But that's why we use functions or at least things like functions So like we used varia we can use variables to get rid of copying and pasting to some extent Mostly variables is there so like if you needed to change a value as you write you would just change it in one location Or you can use variables if you want the program to like change your value based on some conditions With functions it's it is for one it's just gonna clean up clutter and stuff like that it's also going to make it easier on the programmer ... We don't need to talk about the starting and the ending angle here because we're going to we're always going to use the same values here it's always going to make a full circle So we really just want the x the y size in the color so that's exactly what i'm gonna write here x y size color Then what we want to do is take this code here and i'm just gonna cut it paste it then i'm gonna highlight here and i'm going to i was gonna try to have that there we go hit tab and tab it over So now that we've done that The next thing is we need to fix these variables in here So like right now that's just hard coded and this is part of what we wanted to fix So we're actually just gonna pass x y size and then in here we're gonna just put in color So now you've got this blob function

3 setInterval

```javascript
let x = 50;
let y = 50;
function blob(xloc, yloc, size, color){
      context.clearRect(0,0,canvas.width, canvas.height);
      context.beginPath();
      context.arc(xloc,yloc,size,0,2*Math.PI);
      context.fillstyle = color;
      context.fill();
      context.stroke();
      x++;
      y++;
}
setInterval(function(){
      blob(x, y, 20, "green");
}, 100);
```

What happens is when you send in a function with parameters the parameters become a local to the setInterval And so it becomes local to the timer function itself so So now you're like well that's screwed up because well first of all i don't i'm not sure why that's happening I think i'm not sure why that's happening i think that's kind of lame because how like this is so much cleaner than what we're gonna have to do But the workaround is to just make a i'm gonna call it a throwaway function I don't know if there's a particular name for these in JavaScript but it's a throwaway function Literally rather than sending in blob i'm going to send in off just function empty parms and i'm just going to create the function inside here it's i think that's all my way around it I don't know there's there might be something better and if you know a better way please feel free to leave it below So anyways so now what we might think is well what we still can't just like sending in blob here is not going to make any difference so If we send in blob here and do this we can test it but i don't believe that will change anything for us right So it's still not working because it's actually just gonna draw a blob in the same location every single time Oh well definitely let's at least get it somewhere right I just already know it it was gonna fail Oh no it's actually working what the heck

4 Conditionals

```
let x = 50;
let y = 50;
let xChange = 1;
let yChange = 1;
function blob(xloc, yloc, size, color){
      context.clearRect(0,0,canvas.width, canvas.height);
      context.beginPath();
      context.arc(xloc,yloc,size,0,2*Math.PI);
      context.fillstyle = color;
      context.fill();
      context.stroke();
      if (x >= canvas.width || x <= 0){
            xChange *= -1;
      }
      if (y >= canvas.height || y <= 0){
            yChange *= -1;
      }
      x += xChange;
      y += yChange;
}
```

파이썬 프로그래밍 **코딩영어**

So in this case really what we'd want to say we need like some sort of switch that's gonna flip back and forth So instead what we might say is so we've got x and y but then we also let's add a let xChange and we'll say that's equal to 1 Let yChange we'll make that equal to 1 then we'll come down here and rather than do this we'll say x plus equals xChange I'm gonna leave y at 0 for now and now it will say we can kind of clear this up and we really can just close it at this point and then we would say x really if it's greater than or equal to the canvas width what we want to say is xChange equals negative 1 right and then you could go back the other way and flip it around both i'll talk about that in a moment So really what we want to do is actually just flip xChange So the way i would do that is every to if you want to flip something every single time you can just do times equals negative 1 so if xChange is negative 1 well it's negative 1 times negative 1 positive 1 if it's a positive 1 positive 1 times negative 1 is negative 1 so this will flip it back and forth every single time So now if i save this and we just leave this as xChange we run that it should bounce back the other way and then it goes back off the other screen again

5 Object Oriented Programming

```
class Blob {
      constructor(*color, size){    //this is your init
            this.x = Math.random() * canvas.width
            this.y = Math.random() * canvas.height
            this.color = color
            this.size = size
            this.xChange = 1;
            this.yChange = 1;
      }
      move(){
            if(this.x >= canvas.width || this.x <= 0){
                  this.xChange *= -1
            }
            if(this.y >= canvas.height || this.y <= 0){
                  this.yChange *= -1
            }
            this.x += this.xChange;
            this.y += this.yChange;
      }
      // don't wanna clear per a blob draw
      draw(){
            context.beginPath();
            context.arc(this.x, this.y,this.size, 0, 2*Math.PI);
            context.fillStyle = this.color;
            context.fill();
            context.stroke();
      }
}
```

```
const newBlob = new Blob("green",25)
newBlob.draw();
newBlob.move();
newBlob.draw();              // ...etc.
```

But the first method is called your constructor method Now this is the one that if when you define your object if you wanted to be a little pass certain values these are where you're gonna pass them So you'll notice i didn't put you know parentheses here(*) It's not because i forgot it's because actually they go here(*) So in your constructor method we're gonna pass color in size and then the code to the method So it looks a lot like a function Now the only big difference is basically with this constructor method Anytime you define a blob object the constructor method will be run So in this case anything we put in here(*) is going to be run Now generally what you actually put in here are the attributes So we're gonna have the attributes like x and well i don't know why i didn't in Anyway x and y and color in size These are the things that are gonna go in here Now in order to make these attributes accessible across the entire objects we actually lead them with a this I don't it's not a keyword i don't think i'm not really sure what to call this word Some JavaScript expert that's watching these tutorials for some reason can comment below Anyway we lead them with this and it just refers to this object So we're just gonna say this dot x this dot y this dot color and this dot size It's like self in Python

6) For loops

```javascript
const colors = new
Array("red","green","blue","yellow","orange","purple","pink");
let blobs = new Array();

class Blob {
        constructor(color, size){     // this is your init
...
        }
        move(){
...
        }
        // don't wanna clear per a blob draw
        draw(){
...
        }
}
for (let i = 0; i<10; i++){
        let randColor = randomChoice(colors)
        let newBlob = new Blob(randColor,25);
        blobs.push(newBlob);
}
function canvasDraw(){
        context.clearRect(0, 0, canvas.width, canvas.height);
        blobs.forEach(function(obj){
                obj.draw();
                obj.move();
        })
}
```

```
function randomChoice(arr){
        return arr[Math.floor(Math.random() * arr.length)];
}
setInterval(canvasDraw, 10);
```

Now once we've done the clearRect now we want to draw all of the blobs that we know about Now the forEach loop is super useful for this We could use a for loop here but i'm gonna use a forEach loop and the way that we're gonna do that is basically you're gonna say the object that you want to iterate over Now obviously this object needs to be iterable So in this case blobs is the array that has four blobs but we're going to say blobs dot forEach and then we want to do this thing Now in this case the thing that we want to do is a couple of things So instead because every time we draw a blob we actually want to move the blob Now we could in theory if that was always gonna be true rather than having the draw Like every time we draw we could at the end of draw run a move like every time we drew it But later like we that might not be something we want to do every single time we draw it Like maybe the blob holds still for some reason So we don't necessarily want that So that's why in this case you don't always have to you know do a forEach and then run some sort of function But in our case that's what we want to do So we're gonna say function and then the parameter to this function will be just object Now this could be anything It could be blob we're just giving a temporary name to each of the elements in blobs so each element in the blobs is a blob object So you can call it blob You call obj You could call it this like It really doesn't matter

① Introduction

우리의 project name은 mysite, 거기에 또 다른 mysite가 나오는데 그건 primary app이라 부르기로 해서 이 둘을 구분한다. command mode 에서 >py manage.py startapp main이라 해서 main core directory를 만들어 내고선 primary app mysite에 있는 urls.py를 복제해서 main에도 하나 만들어 낸다. 그리곤 primary app mysite의 urls.py에선 path(' ', include ('main.urls')) 라고 해서 main의 urls.py를 찾게 해 주고선, main의 urls.py에다 path 문에서 또 한 번 더 main 의 views.homepage를 찾아가게 해서 거기서 최종 우리의 홈페이지를 보여 준다.

```
two different names of mysite .... primary app(inner) vs
project(outer)

"""pramary app mysite URL Configuration"""
from django.contrib import admin
from django.urls import path, include

urlpatterns = [
        path('', include('main.urls')),
        path('admin/', admin.site.urls),
]

"""main URL Configuration"""
from django.urls import path
from . import views
app_name = "main"
urlpatterns = [
        path("", views.homepage, name="homepage"),
]
```

```
"""main views.py"""
from django.shortcuts import render
from django.http import HttpResponse
# Create your views here.
def homepage(request):
  return HttpResponse("Wow this is an
<strong>awesome<strong> tutorial")
```

So i'm gonna go into first let's go to mysite urls dot py so primary app I switched around don't get confused it's your fault So what we want to do here is we just need to take this because it's our primary app and point it to our new app called main So we're gonna add another path here I'm just gonna copy this come down here and i'm gonna paste and then what i'm gonna say is We're gonna well first let's also import include and then what we're gonna say for this path is an empty path So homepage no other urls are being submitted here We want to include main dot urls So whenever someone comes to just the homepage and there's nothing else that this path is gonna match So then it's gonna say okay let's go to main dot urls now So then we're gonna go to main urls Make sure you're in main urls And now what we want to do is actually we don't need admin here so i'm gonna delete that for now and then we are gonna say and we don't need this admin either We'll keep path and then the other thing we're gonna do is from just relative import views and then we're gonna pass an app name and we're gonna say appname equals main This is useful later on when you're trying to create custom urls that will point to a specific view But you don't actually have to hard code the urls it's all totally dynamic So right now we're not using that but i just don't want to forget about it later And you might as well just always throw this in because eventually you'll want to have that functionality and you'll try to use it Because you saw it in an example somewhere or something and it's not gonna work and you're gonna be like wait what? So anyway, we'll throw that in there for now

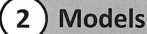

2 Models

우리가 쓰는 data base에다 어떤 모델을 우리가 쓰고자 하는지를 정해 주어야 합니다. 이 학습은 과거 flask web framework로 서비스 중이었던 Pythonprogramming.net site를 Django로 바꾸어 낸 실제 사례입니다. 사소한 관리마저도 손을 거쳐야 하는 flask와는 달리 Django web framework에선 웬만한 건 알아서 시스템에서 처리해 주니 유지 보수에 한결 수월하다 합니다. class Tutorial(models.Model): 이라고 우린 tutorial model을 상속받아 쓰겠다고 클래스 선언을 합니다. 그리고 나서 table을 만들어 내는 일을 합니다. 두 수순을 밟아야 하는데 하나가 makemigration 그리고 나머지 하나가 migrate 입니다. 우린 makemigration을 해내려면, 먼저 primary app mysite의 settings.py 에다 MainConfig app을 등록해 주고, main apps.py에 그게 등록되어 있는지를 확인부터 해야 합니다.

```
C:\Users\UseDesktop\mysite>python manage.py runserver
...>python manage.py makemigrations
No changes detected

"""mysite settings.py"""
#Application definition
INSTALLED_APPS = [
      'main.apps.MainConfig',
]

"""main apps.py"""
from django.apps import AppConfig
class MainConfig(AppConfig):
      name = 'main'

>python manage.py makemigrations
```

```
Migrations for, 'main':
     main \migrations/0001...initial.py ... Create model
Tutorial

>python manage.py migrate
Operations to perform:
Apply all migrations: admin, auth, contenttypes, main, sessions
Running migrations:
```

So every time you make a new model that's a new table therefore you have to do two things with Django One you have to do a thing called make migrations and all that does is kind of prepare your migrations Then you have to actually migrate So it's two steps So as you've seen already when we run our server i'm assuming one is still running Nope I guess i'm not running a server anymore So python manage dot py run server It was giving us a message before Let's see what it does this time Starting development server at http://127.0.0.1:8000/ okay So it says you know you we need to probably run a migrate This is really only like because we just made this website that we want to run this So what i'm gonna do i guess cd what do we call this mysite right mysite yes So i think it's in here So what we can do is i just i hate that i'm just gonna do it in order that you're supposed to do it We'll do the other migrations at the same time because there's only one time you'll run that migrate first So what we're gonna say here is basically every time you add or change So if you add another model or you want to change a pre-existing model you have to make migrations then migrate And that's basically it unless you happen to hit an error So we've made this new model so the first thing i want us to do is make migrations So we're just gonna say python manage dot py makemigrations and it says No changes detected So what happened here The reason why i really did do this on purpose You're gonna hit this and if i did it didn't hit it for you You would be stumped or at least if you're like me and you're slow You would be stumped for a few minutes So what happens is anytime you start a new app We were able to point to that new app but we haven't like installed that new app So first we have to install that new app in order for it to add tables to our database I'm not really sure the design reason why

3 Admin & Apps

사이트 관리를 위해선 admin 즉 superuser가 필요하고, console에서 python manage.py createsuperuser 해 등록합니다. 127.0.0.1:8000/admin 모드에선 user 관리뿐만 아니라 우리가 장고 models.Model에서 상속받아 만든 Tutorial 관리 기능까지를 필요로 합니다. 그렇게 하기 위해선 main admin.py엘 가서 Tutorial을 등록해 주어야 하고, define class TutorialAdmin(admin.ModelAdmin):같이 admin.ModelAdmin을 override 하고 등록해서 customizing도 가능케 해 줍니다. 특별히 우리가 만들고 있는 건 프로그래밍 tutorial이라 TextField의 coding syntax를 highlight 해서 잘 드러나 보이게 해 주는 것이 중요하고 필요합니다. project urls.py 에서 path tinymce를 넣어 주고, main admin.py와 primary app mysite settings.py 에서 각기 models.TextField를 'widget': TinyMCE( )로 formfield override 하고, app을 INSTALLED_APPS에다 등록해 주면 그게 가능하게 됩니다.

```
C:\Users\USER\Desktop\mysite>python manage.py
createsuperuser

"""main admin.py:"""
from django.contrib import admin
from .models import Tutorial
from tinymce.widgets import TinyMCE
from django.db import models


#Register your models here.
class TutorialAdmin(admin.ModelAdmin):
    fieldsets = [
            ("Title/date", {"fields": ["tutorial_title",
            "tutorial_published"]}),
            ("Content", {"fields": ["tutorial_content"]})
```

```
]
        formfield_overrides = {
            models.TextField: {'widget': TinyMCE()}
}
admin.site.register(Tutorial, TutorialAdmin)
```

Now i know you must be wondering well what about our model because we just made a model in the last tutorial where's that at Well you have to register your models So you go to the Django registration you cut out a little piece of the cardboard that your Django package came in to correct myself oh okay So what we got to do is go into main and we just go into admin here and in fact i told myself i was gonna keep using this one So we go here and register your models here So all we have to do is actually import the tutorial models So from models import tutorial don't forget the relative period there And then all we need to do is admin dot site dot register and we could do tutorial like that tutorial hopefully I spelled that right let's find out let's refresh boom Tutorials interestingly enough this has an s appended to it even though the you know tutorial is singular I forget what it is There is a method you can override eventually we will probably hit it but it because it's kind of annoying so a turn like series what it's going to do this just adds an s to it It doesn't have any handling for If the thing ends an s maybe do like es or just a an apostrophe es so it doesn't it's really stupid it just adds an s So anyway later what we can fix that But that's where the s is coming from it's literally taking the model name plus s So yeah but later on down the line when you're like trying to go back and figure out where is it getting the name from? that's what's going on So anyway been there done that ok so That's how we could register it super simple and if we click on tutorials boom We can already see the tutorial that we actually made and all the fields are here and notice how like you the date published has this thing like today and now and you could click on a calendar and pick all these things are done for us And like for example here this is charfield and it's just like ... a lot of stuff went into this and that's pretty awesome

4 Views & Templates

Really the way that most of your pages are going to be served is via all the things to do with the MVC or model view controller framework 사이트가 서브되기 위해선 MVC model, view templates, controller for the urls가 필요합니다. 이번 강좌는 이 세 framework를 모두 같이 들여다보는 첫 기회가 되겠습니다. 앞으론 project mysite, primary app mysite, main core main dir 등을 번거롭게 일일이 기록하지 않겠습니다. sublime text3 에서 file - open folder를 선택하면 directory별로 가지런히 드러나게 해 주니까요. 원칙만 알고 나면 헷갈릴 일이 없어요. 이번 4강에선 main views.py에서 찾게 해 주는 각종 templates를 위해 main dir 아래에 templates dir를, 그리고 그 아래 또 하나의 main dir를 만들어 냅니다.

우린 이미 models.py에서 우리의 database table을 만들고, migrate 해서 등록을 마쳤습니다. 그리고 직전 강의에서 등록한 admin/superuser 기능으로 admin mode엘 들어가 print tutorial이란 데이터 entry를 하나 더 추가했습니다. 그리고 우리의 입맛에 맞게 테이블을 다시 디자인하고, Textfield엔 code syntax를 잘 보여 주는 tinymce 모듈을 가져와 적용했습니다. 이제 일반 user들이 들어왔을 때 과연 우리 사이트가 어떻게 보여지는지를 살피는 단계입니다.

main urls.py는 views.homepage로 안내하는 데에서 달라지는 게 없습니다. 우린 views.py를 갔을 때 define homepage function에서 return render 문으로 template_name="main/home.html",로 가게 해 줍니다. 즉, 프로그램 control이 template dir 그리고 거기 안에 있는 main dir를 찾아가서 각종 .html 파일을 뒤져 화면을 뿌려 주게 합니다.

문제가 되었던 것이 admin/superuser 모드에서 print tutorial 데이터레코드를 하나 새롭게 만들면서 우린 tinymce라는 code syntax가 잘 드러나는 편집기를 사용하고 settings.py에다 app 등록까지 마쳤었는데 그게 반영이 되질 않았어요. 하지만 home.html에서 {% load static %} <link href="{% static 'tinymce/css/prism.css' %}" rel="stylesheet"> 라고 static files를 부르고, CSS, JavaScript 문을 넣어 줌으로써 반영되어 잘 보이게 해결을 보았습니다.

```
"""models.py:"""
class Tutorial(models.Model):
      tutorial_title = models.CharField(max_length=200)
      tutorial_content = models.TextField()
      tutorial_published = models.DateTimeField("date
published", default=datetime.now())
      def __str__(self):
            return self.tutorial_title


"""views.py:"""
def homepage(request):
      return render(request=request,
                    template_name="main/home.html",
                    context={"tutorials": Tutorial.objects.all})


"""home.html:"""
{% load static %}
<link href="{% static 'tinymce/css/prism.css' %}"
rel="stylesheet">
<script src="{% static 'tinymce/js/prism.js' %}"></script>

"""main urls.py:"""
from . import views
app_name = "main"
urlpatterns = [
      path("", views.homepage, name="homepage"),
```

So the next thing is you might be wondering hey that's not looking like what we had in the admin 127 and then there we go If we click on tutorial we go to the print tutorial for example what happened to this beautiful syntax highlighting that we had what gives bro Well what we need here is some CSS cascading style sheet and also some JavaScript So what we're gonna do is bring in both and Since we're at home dot html we'll just do it all in this same file So the first thing is for statics so first of all the CSS already exists It was when we grabbed the tinyMCE app We actually got there CSS So we're actually just gonna use theirs and it's already here Now to use something from our static directory the first thing we need to do is load static unlike like flask for example if you're familiar The static directory is always accessible in flask whereas in Django if you go to slash static you won't find a directory there it's not like publicly accessible basically All the stuff in static is in Django accessible you just not gonna find a like a directory structure like you would in flask I'm sure you can hide it in flasks I just it's never been important enough to me to worry about it but anyways So now what we want to do is we want to add that style sheet So we're gonna add a link here and in here is where we care going to pass some more logics So again just like this was logic here you can also use logic in string form So in this case this is kind of some weird logic that you'll type nothing really else is gonna act like this Oh actually probably what i want to do i think we would get away with this act either way but i'm gonna use single quotes here just so we don't So the html itself doesn't look funky But this is where we are gonna specify the location so and this would be already in a static directory just like template static is loaded in the same way it's slash static So again the handling is no different than the way that we handle for here right It's already looking for a templates directory So it's gonna look for the app name and then the actual template The same thing is true with static writes app name and then if you had further directories sure

⑤ Styling/CSS

사이트의 모양새를 내기 위해 필요로 하는 제반 모듈들을 제공하는 materialize 혹은 material design이라 부르는 프레임워크가 있습니다. 이미지 처리, CSS, JavaScript 거의 모든 기능들이 모듈별로 잘 정리되어 제공되고 있습니다. 그냥 코드들을 갖다 써도 되고, 컬러 같은 경우엔 koala라는 materialize Sass source를 컴파일 해 주는 compiler로 컴파일해서 바로 쓸 수 있는 load module 형태로 저장해 두었다 쓸 수도 있습니다. 실습에선 두 가지 경우를 다 보여 줍니다.

먼저 화면을 side by side, 기기별로 size에 따라 각기 다르게 보여 주는 기능을 row라 하고, CSS component cards에 올린 사례를 가져와서 수정해 우리의 Tutorial을 보여 줄 수 있게 만들었습니다. 페이지 상단에 보여 주는 타이틀 라인은 Navbar라고 해서 별도로 body문 바로 아래에다 넣어 줍니다. 그러곤 Django의 extends and includes 기능으로 home.html의 요체를 이루는(truly unique) 기능을 제외하곤 나머지 모두를 header.html로 옮겨 가서 각기 전문화된 코딩만을 담고 관리하게 합니다.

```
{% extends "main/header.html" %}
{% block content %}
    <div class="row">
    {% for tut in tutorials %}
        <div class="col s12 m6 l4">
            <div class="card blue-grey darken-1">
                <div class="card-content white-text">
                    <span class="card-
    title">{{tut.tutorial_title}}</span>
                    <p style="font-
            size:70%">{{tut.tutorial_published}}</p>
                    <p>{{tut.tutorial_content|safe}}</p>
                    <div class="card-action">
                        <a href="#">Visit</a>
```

```
                    </div>
                </div>
              </div>
            </div>
        {% endfor %}
        </div>
    {% endblock %}
```

이어지는 컬러링 작업을 우린 Sass로 합니다. Sass(Syntactically Awesome Style Sheets)는 CSS pre-processor로서 CSS의 한계와 단점을 보완해서 보다 가독성이 높고 코드의 재사용에 유리한 CSS를 생성하기 위한 CSS의 확장(extension) 이라 합니다. 암튼 우린 이 Sass source를 받아 내는 동안에 한쪽에선 그 소스를 컴파일할 koala Sass라는 모듈을 또 다운로드 받습니다. 이 작업은 한참이 걸립니다. 그 사이에 Sass source download가 먼저 끝났습니다. 우린 zip file을 풀어 가지고선 거기 components color-variables.scss 파일을 customize 합니다. 우리가 원하는 색깔을 primary colors인 $materialize-red: 등에다 지정해 줍니다. 요령은 google 에서 html hex color 치면 나오는 color picker를 활용해서 원하는 컬러로 $materialize-red: 등을 customize 해 줍니다. 그러는 사이에 koala 다운로드가 끝났습니다. 여기선 compile할 파일(materialize-src-v1.0.0)을 + 를 눌러 선택해 주면 되고, 그렇게 해서 나온 customized 된 새로운 CSS 파일인 materialize를 우리의 project module 들이 있는 directory mysite - main - static - main - CSS 안에다 옮겨 줍니다. 그리곤 우리의 header.html에서

```
{% load static %}
    <!-- Compiled and minified CSS -->
    <link href="{% static 'main/css/materialize.css' %}"
rel="stylesheet">
```

이라고 넣어 주면 우리의 홈페이지에 반영이 되어 나옵니다.

The other thing i want to talk about is changing the actual design here So what i'm going to do is we'll come over to materialize CSS and if you want to customize this go ahead and code that main site hit get started Maybe there we go i did click it and what we want is this Sass So go ahead and click on that source And then while you're waiting on that we're gonna go ahead and grab Koala Sass probably You need something that's gonna compile the Sass So i'll grab that hopefully it doesn't take us too long to install it I seem to have recollection that one time this took a while But i'll at least talk you guys through it and then i'll also be hosting at least the Sass file but then also i could probably host the materialize that CSS file as well but i want you guys to understand like how it's done So in the old days you would have to go through an like you know find and replace which is not ideal So instead what you can do is Sass is you just modify a couple of variables instead and or in this case quite a few variables and but it's a lot easier than finding and replacing and then there's like certain ones that you happen to miss and you're like ah shucks and that's exactly what you say is shucks So while that's installing that does look like it's gonna take a while please go faster okay So let me extract all here okay cool So this is from materialize so if i go to source if i go to source i'll come into here Basically once Koala where did it go you'll come into Sass actually probably preloads the actual Sass file that you need but in this but what you need to do first is come into Sass directory Let me just scroll in here and then probably components and the we're looking for color color variables So we will open that with sublime text great

6 User registration

Django user model을 활용해 내는 단원입니다.

```
mysite>python manage.py shell
>>> from Django.contrib.auth.models import User
>>> dir(User)
```

장고엔 이미 User model이 만들어져 제공되고 있으며, 여기서 우린 수많은 dunder methods가 사용 가능하게 제공되고 있음을 볼 수 있습니다.

우리 사이트엘 들어가면 맨 처음 보여 주는 페이지 Navbar엔 Home Register, Login이 나옵니다. 이제 거기서 Register를 선택했을 때 나오는 register.html을 만드는 순서입니다.

```
{% block content %}
    <form method="POST">
        {% csrf_token %}
        {{form}}
        If you already have an account, <a
href="/login"><strong>login</strong></a> instead.
{% endblock %}
```

이제 이 html page를 point 해 줄 view가 필요하겠죠?

```
def register(request):
    form = UserCreationForm
    return render(request,
                    "main/register.html",
                    context={"form":form})
```

model은 우리 Django에서 제공한 User란 model을 쓰니깐 따로 만들 필요가 없어요. 그러니 마지막 순서가 controller 즉, urls.py입니다.

```
urlpatterns = [
        path("", views.homepage, name="homepage"),
        path("register/", views.register, name="register")
]
```

이렇게 해서 MVC(model, view, controller)가 모두 세팅되었습니다. 확인해 보실까요?
http://127.0.0.1:800/register 해서 들어갑니다. 움스, 화면이 꽉 차서 여유가 없어요. header.html
에서 우리 block을 넘어갈 때 container 옵션을 주어서 여유있게 내용을 볼 수 있게 해 줍니다.

```
<div class="container">
    <br>
    {% block content %}
    {% endblock %}
</div>
```

register.html을 보완해서 register 버튼이 작동되게 만듭니다.

```
    {{form.as_p}}
    <button class="btn" style="background-color:yellow;
color:blue" type="submit">register</button>
</form>
```

자, 이렇게 해서 다시 http://127.0.0.1:8000/register엘 들어가서 register를 시도해 보지만, 여전히

아무런 반응이 없습니다. 왜일까요? views.py에 올린 def register(request):에서 default request 인 getrequest가 작동했기 때문입니다. 우린 if 조건문을 넣어서 postrequest 일 때 해야 할 행동을 따로 정의해 주어야 합니다.

```python
if request.method == "POST":
    form = UserCreationForm(request.POST)

if form.is_valid():
    user = form.save()
    username = form.cleaned_data.get('username')
    messages.success(request, f"New account created:
{username}")
    login(request, user)
    messages.info(request, f"You are now logged in as
{username}")
    return redirect("main:homepage")
else:
    for msg in form.error_messages:
        messages.error(request, f"{msg}:
{form.error_messages[msg]}")
```

자, 이젠 다시 우리의 홈페이지엘 들어가셔서 새로운 user를 하나 만들어 보시고, 그게 작동하는지를 확인하심 끝나게 되겠습니다.

And we hit register we see nothing happens why did nothing happen? Well if we come to views dot py we look at register this request a default request is a get request So as we come through here we're just handling basically for the get request So the problem is this from creates a post request which is a little more dangerous Well in one case people are just trying to get the server to give them some information In other case we're trying to let the user submit some information to our server like make changes often with the post So what we need to do now is make is actually handle for the post request in our register function So the way that we're going to do that is form usercreationform Actually i think in both cases hmm no Because in this case it's like a blank form and the other one it's like the form from the request So actually this will just make totally separate and what we're going to say here is someone was complaining to and one of the like the first video the text was not big enough I've zoomed it in quite a bit but feel free to leave a comment below and tell me if the zoom is still unacceptable I just hate making it huge because then text runs off the screen Anyway if request dot method is a POST as a PSOT oh my gosh I even got it right okay If request method is POST then our form it equals and it is UserCreationForm but it's populated with request dot post So then what we can do is we want to check to see is the form valid So if form dot is valid meaning things are filled out in the way that they're supposed to be filled out So if the form is valid we're gonna say user equals form dot save This is equivalent of the dot save for the user So at this point if the form was valid, so if the user doesn't it already exists all that stuff we create the user So form dot save save is the equivalent of like model dot save okay So boom the user has been created

7 Messages & includes

각기 웹 프레임워크들마다 자신의 유니크한 메시지를 사이트에 내보내고 있습니다. Django에서도 마찬가지. views.py에서 from django.contrib import messages를 해 주고선 register/login한 user의 username 정도라도 간략하게 message에 담습니다. 그러곤 materializecss.com엘 가서 찾은 JavaScript M.toast 기능으로 간단히 각기 색깔을 달리해서 2초간 pop up message로 register 혹은 login한 username을 알려 줍니다. 이때 이 내용을 register.html 에 담지 않고, header.html에다 담는 것을 유의바람. message를 쏟아 내는 내용은 register에만 국한되는 건 아니기 때문입니다. 새로운 user를 하나 register 함으로써 message pop up 기능이 작동하는 지를 확인합니다.

역시 header.html에 올란 Navbar에 나오는 버튼을 account/Logout, register/Login으로 다시 조정해 줍니다. 이제 복잡해진 header.html을 깔끔하니 정리해 줄 때가 왔습니다. {% include "main/includes/navbar.html" %}

{% include "main/includes/messages.html" %}라 하고선 각기 navbar.html, messages.html을 새로 만들어서 해당 모듈을 copy - paste 해서 templates/main/includes dir 에다 위치시켜 줍니다. 이제 header.html이 아래와 같이 깔끔하니 정리되어 나왔습니다.

```html
<head>
    {% load static %}
        <link href="{% static 'tinymce/css/prism.css' %}"
    rel="stylesheet">
        <!-- Compiled and minified CSS -->
        <link href="{% static 'main/css/materialize.css' %}"
    rel="stylesheet">
        <!-- Compiled and minified JavaScript -->
        <script
    src="https://cdnjs.cloudflare.com/.../1.0.0/js/materialize.min.
    js"></script>
```

```
</head>
<body>
    {% include "main/includes/navbar.html" %}
    {% include "main/includes/messages.html" %}
    <div class="container">
        <br>
        {% block content %}
        {% endblock %}
    </div>
</body>
<script src="{% static 'tinymce/js/prism.js' %}"></script>
```

LC training(13:32)

The next thing i'd like to do is just show a different looking navigation bar once the user has logged in So the next thing we're gonna do is coming back to our header dot html and we'll come over to our nav bar which is all right here So we would still i mean the logo should stay the same home button can stay the same but really here this should be different depending on these two things should be different depending on if the user is logged in or not So what we can ask is if user dot is authenticated if user is authenticated we show something else and then we will end whoops and endif statement So i'm just going to take this tab it over copy come down here oops tab that over copy paste okay So if the user is authenticated they're logged in they don't need to register anymore They might have i don't know an account page So may be head to slash account and then we could even call this their username So i think user dot username would probably work here I don't really actually know i think that's probably good enough and then here rather than login it should be logout Maybe we'll capitalize that L as well okay all right So now let us head back on over let's refresh okay cool So now it shows the username and Logout because this user is logged in Now we don't actually have Logout handling yet We will probably do that in the next tutorial

8 User Login/out

user login/out 기능을 만들어 줍니다. User Model을 쓰고, Views.py와 login.html, forms.py 작업을 요하고, controller urls.py에다 path를 만들어 줘야 합니다.

```
path("logout/", views.logout_request, name="logout"),
path("login/", views.login_request, name="login")
]
```

MVC(model, view, controller)의 원칙을 따라가면 그리 혼란스럽지가 않답니다.

실습에선 먼저 urls.py에다 Logout/in path를 만들어 줍니다. 그러곤 views.py로 가서 logout_request/login_request function을 만들어 냅니다. 여기서 login_request syntax는 이전 단원에서 실습했던 register의 경우랑 거의 동일합니다. getrequest와 postrequest의 두 가지 경우를 공히 처리해줍니다.

```
def login_request(request):
    if request.method == "POST":
        form = AuthenticationForm(request, data=request.POST)
        if form.is_valid():
            username = form.cleaned_data.get('username')
            password = form.cleaned_data.get('password')
            user = authenticate(username=username,
            password=password)
            if user is not None:
                login(request, user)
                messages.info(request, f"You are now logged in
as {username}")
```

```
            return redirect("main:homepage")
        else:
            messages.error(request, "Invalid username or
password")
    else:
        messages.error(request, "Invalid username or
password")
    form = AuthenticationForm()
    return render(request,
                  "main/login.html",
                  {"form":form})
```

자, forms 관련해서 마지막 터치가 남았습니다. UserCreationForm은 정형적인 형식의 폼을 주고
받는 용도입니다만, 우린 자기 사이트만의 특별한 field를 추가로 받고자 이 form을 변경해서 적용
해 보고 싶은 사정도 있을 겁니다. 그땐 따로 forms.py라고 UserCreationForm을 상속받은 별도
의 Class object를 만들어서 활용해 내는 것이 편리합니다. 실습에선 email을 하나 더 추가해서
user를 등록해 내는 케이스입니다.

```
from django import forms
from django.contrib.auth.forms import UserCreationForm
from django.contrib.auth.models import User

class NewUserForm(UserCreationForm):
    email = forms.EmailField(required=True)

    class Meta:
        model = User
        fields = ("username", "email", "password1", "password2")

    def save(self, commit=True):
        user = super(NewUserForm, self).save(commit=False)
        user.email = self.cleaned_data['email']
        if commit:
            user.save()
        return user
```

So now what we have to do is same thing for register we can fill out this form own we could hit login But nothing's gonna happen because we're not handling for When the method is a post request So it's just like with the registration the bulk of the code is gonna be involved if the method is a POST and in fact i'm gonna go ahead and just copy that Boop come on down here and we're gonna get ready for the login request So if the request method equals POST we're going to say form is again an authentication form with request in then request dot post pat lovely So here request is just always passed I don't know if i quit stop post um I'm not really sure we talked about this This would just be your data though This is just so it knows what data is like for that form whoops like that Actually since that's a parameter probably doesn't have spaces Anyways that's what that parameter is I think that's pretty obvious So once we have so we've got the form here with the information and then if form dot and then again is valid what we want to grab is the username that's gonna be something and we want to get the password that's gonna be something Because when someone logs in we have to be able to authenticate that user so here is where we're going to use authenticate and if everything is hunkey-dory we could log them in So coming on down here username that will be du be du form dot to get clean I'm sorry that's not it form dot cleaned data yes And then the field name in this case is username So that's kind of what i mean Right now this is kind of black box too because you're like I don't know what i would put through here But this is the field name So you know if we were to open up the code for authenticate form for example it's got multiple fields well two username password and so and then it has the name of that field like if you're gonna build that filled out in Let's say html you would have that name and that you would do the same thing to get that parameter

9 Linking models

여기부터가 linking models, foreign keys 토픽입니다. Django를 하시는 분들이 다들 여기서 나가떨어진다 합니다. 정신 바짝 차리고 따라오시기 바랍니다.

1,200개에 달하는 tutorials를 어떻게 해야 한 곳 사이트에다 다 담을 수가 있을까요? 예, 카테고리별로 분류해서 차곡차곡 담아야 하지 않을까요? 그리고 하나의 model 즉, 데이터베이스 테이블에다 다 담는 것보다는 여러 개의 데이터베이스 테이블을 관리해 내는 것이 카테고리 관리에 유리하지 않을까요? 그 기법으로 소요되는 것이 foreign keys 입니다.

models.py엘 들어가서 class Tutorial에 이어 TutorialCategory(attributes - tutorial_category, category_summary, category_slug), TutorialSeries(attributes - tutorial_series, tutorial_category with foreign key, series_summary) 두 개를 더 models.Model을 상속받아 만들어 냅니다. 그리곤 처음에 만들었던 Tutorial class엘 가서 url을 연결할 목적의 tutorial_slug와, point Tutorial to TutorialSeries 목적의 tutorial_series with foreign key라는 두 개의 attributes를 더 만들어 줍니다.

```python
class TutorialCategory(models.Model):
    tutorial_category = models.CharField(max_length=200)
    category_summary = models.CharField(max_length=200)
    category_slug = models.CharField(max_length=200)
    class Meta:
        verbose_name_plural = "Categories"
    def __str__(self):
        return self.tutorial_category


class TutorialSeries(models.Model):
    tutorial_series = models.CharField(max_length=200)
    tutorial_category = models.ForeignKey(TutorialCategory,
default=1, verbose_name="Category",
on_delete=models.SET_DEFAULT)
```

```
    series_summary = models.CharField(max_length=200)
    class Meta:
        verbose_name_plural = "Series"
    def __str__(self):
        return self.tutorial_series


# Create your models here.
class Tutorial(models.Model):
    tutorial_title = models.CharField(max_length=200)
    tutorial_content = models.TextField()
    tutorial_published = models.DateTimeField("date
published", default=datetime.now())

    # point Tutorial to TutorialSeries
    tutorial_series = models.ForeignKey(TutorialSeries,
default=1, verbose_name="Series",
on_delete=models.SET_DEFAULT)
    tutorial_slug = models.CharField(max_length=200,
default=1)
    def __str__(self):
        return self.tutorial_title
```

이어서 makemigrations, migrate 하다 indentation 에러가 발생했어요. 구글링을 해서 How to Reset Migrations By Vitor Freitas라는 좋은 tutorial을 찾아 먼저 자신감을 갖고선, models.py, views.py 파일을 old version 으로 환원 시킨 후 debugging을 해 문제 발생한 곳이 forms.py에서 모든 코드들이 (어쩐 일인지 모르지만) tab 하나씩 indent가 된 것을 찾아내고선 극복할 수 있었습니다. 전 실험 중인 상황이니 db를 없애고 전혀 새롭게 시작해도 되는 상황이라 Scenario 1의 1-3을 밟았고, 비교적 수월하게 처리해 낼 수 있었습니다. 휴, 다행!

Scenario 1:

The project is still in the development environment and you want to perform a full clean up. You don't mind throwing the whole database away.

1. Remove all the migrations files within your project

Go through each of your projects apps migration folder and remove everything inside, except the __init__.py file.

Or if you are using a UNIX-like OS you can run the following script (inside your project dir):

find . -path "*/migrations/*.py" -not -name "__init__.py" -delete

find . -path "*/migrations/*.pyc" -delete

2. Drop the current database, or delete the db.sqlite3 if it is your case.

3. Create the initial migrations and generate the database schema:

python manage.py makemigrations

python manage.py migrate

And you are good to go.

마지막 처리해 줘야 할 것이 admin.py에다 몇 가지 db tables를 반영해 주는 일입니다.

```python
from .models import Tutorial, TutorialSeries,
TutorialCategory

    fieldsets = [
        ("Title/date", {"fields": ["tutorial_title",
"tutorial_published"]}),
        ("URL", {"fields": ["tutorial_slug"]}),
        ("Series", {"fields": ["tutorial_series"]}),
        ("Content", {"fields": ["tutorial_content"]})
    ]
admin.site.register(TutorialSeries)
admin.site.register(TutorialCategory)
```

And then finally we need to point tutorial to tutorial series So all we're gonna do We've got title content published We're gonna point here let me just come down here zoom in a little bit okay We're gonna say tutorial underscore series not camel case series equals models models dot foreign key and that foreign key here is the tutorial series that it's a part of the default will be one We'll specify the verbose name as well as the on delete So the verbose name equals series and then on delete We want to models dot set underscore default I just wanna see that with my eyeballs thank you sir All looks good to me Now a tutorial series i'm going to do the same thing i do on Python programming dot net we don't really need a unique url for the tutorial series In my opinion the series is one of two things either when someone clicks on that tutorial series it poops then in to tutorial number one right or if you wanted to get really fancy the last tutorial or the latest tutorial part that that user left off on but that would be dynamic by user So otherwise it's just the first tutorial in the series So that should be good enough So we don't need a url for that But we do need a url for the tutorial itself so i'm gonna add that in and we're gonna say tutorial underscore slug equals models dot you guessed it it's another charfield and we'll say max length equals 200 and here we definitely want to add a default because tutorials already exist When they have a few of them but they do exist So we need to have some sort of default to throw in the ones that exist already

파이썬 프로그래밍 **코딩영어**

(10) Foreign keys

Django는 실전에서 여러분이 얼마든지 자신의 홈페이지 서비스 구축에 바로 적용해 실효를 거둘 수 있는 활용도가 아주 뛰어난 web development framework입니다. 우리의 실습에선 tutorial model에 적용하지만, 이건 곧 여러분께서 기타 다른 목적의 웹사이트 구축 서비스에서도 고스란히 그대로 적용되는 기술입니다. 우린 기본이 튼튼하면 응용은 얼마든지 자유롭게 개성있는 독특한 자신만의 색깔로 가져갈 수가 있습니다!

제일 어렵다고들 하는 이번 로직을 통과해야 합니다. db 테이블을 여기서 저기로 건너 뛰어(hop) 다른 쪽 테이블에 있는 attribute를 갖고선 작업해야 합니다. 그걸 가능케 해 주는 기능이 Foreign Key입니다. 이걸 적용하는 기법을 이해하는 것이 그리 간단치가 않습니다. 하지만 개념을 알면, 이 것도 우린 극복해 낼 수 있답니다! 고지가 바로 저긴데, 예서 말 수는 없지요. 힘내세요!

먼저 실습을 위한 데이터를 올려놓으셔야 합니다. 카테고리 2개, 시리즈 각기 카테고리별로 2개씩 4개, 시리즈물 각기 시리즈별로 2개씩 이상.

single_slug이란 개념이 나옵니다. 이는 우리의 urls가 모두 ../.. 안에 다 들어간다는 의미입니다. ../../..이 아니라는 더 이상의 url '/' 연장이 없다는 의미입니다. 이에는 TutorialCategory 테이블에 속한 category_slug와 Tutorial 테이블에 속한 tutorial_slug 두 종류가 있습니다. TutorialSeries엔 그저 처음 시리즈물에 이어서 계속되는 시리즈물이 나오는 관계로 이 url 성격의 slug가 별도로 필요없다고 보았습니다. 그리고 이제 우리의 홈페이지 초기화면에선 Tutorial 테이블의 tutorial_title 이 아닌 TutorialCategory 테이블의 tutorial_category attribute를 보여 줍니다.

```
""" views.py """
def single_slug(request, single_slug):
categories = [c.category_slug for c in TutorialCategory.objects.all()]
if single_slug in categories:
return HttpResponse(f"{single_slug} is a category!!!")
```

```
        tutorials = [t.tutorial_slug for t in
Tutorial.objects.all()]
    if single_slug in tutorials:
        return HttpResponse(f"{single_slug} is a tutorial!!!")
```

자, 이렇게 해서 우린 홈페이지 초기화면에서 카테고리를 볼 수 있게 되었습니다. 지금은 그 카테고리를 누르면 여긴 카테고리라는 것만 보여 줍니다. 어떻게 바뀌어야 할까요? 어떤 series에 어떤 tutorial이 있다는 걸 보여 줘야 하지 않을까요? 특별히 series에서 처음 나오는 tutorial을 우린 part_one 이라 부르고 tutorial series를 누르면 part one을 보여 주기로 합니다. 그걸 어떻게 구현해 낸다고요? 두 차례의 매칭 절차를 거칩니다. 먼저, series가 같은 tutorial_category를 hop 해서 category slug을 찾아내어 single_slug 라고 이름지어 줍니다. 다음, 그렇게 찾은 single slug 들의 tutorial_series를 모두 hop 해서 그중 tutorial published가 가장 먼저 올란 tutorial slug를 찾아내어 part one이라 하고 보여 줍니다. 여기서 m은 tutorial series의 object입니다.

```
def single_slug(request, single_slug):
    categories = [c.category_slug for c in
TutorialCategory.objects.all()]
    if single_slug in categories:
        matching_series =
TutorialSeries.objects.filter(tutorial_category__category_slug
=single_slug)
        series_urls = {}
        for m in matching_series.all():
            part_one =
Tutorial.objects.filter(tutorial_series__tutorial_series=m.tutorial
_series).earliest("tutorial_published")
            series_urls[m] = part_one.tutorial_slug
        return render(request,
                      "main/category.html",
                      {"part_ones": series_urls})
```

So let's say we know fundamentals is a category Now what well now what we need to be able to do is find all of the tutorials that are in the category where that categories slug is python fundamentals So that's a little challenging because our categories do here the foreign key that is the series but the series then has a foreign key that is the category and then the category has an attribute that's the slug So we have to make a couple of jumps here which would be easier if the category was possibly in the same table as the tutorial But like i said before you wouldn't really want that because your database lookups would be these huge queries and you don't wouldn't want to make that happen So instead what we'll do now is go back to views and and what we want to do yeah Let's say we make a match here so just for the category we want to find the matching tutorial series who's category has a category slug that is what we passed So before i said i think i said tutorial and i was mistaken So really what we're trying to do is we're just trying to find the tutorial series because we want to link to the entire series let's say So in this case the way we're going to do that is matching series equals tutorial series because that's what we're looking for at the end of the day is tutorial series objects dot filter and what we want to fill where we how we want to filter is first like let's open up that models Because this is this is where you're gonna have probably the hardest time yeah so tutorial series How do we go from tutorial series to category slug? Well first we have to make the hop with this foreign key right? We need to find the tutorial category So tutorial series we're gonna filter by category okay which points to tutorial category but we and we want category slug from there So the real questions is how do we make that hop and attributes Because both are not intuitive so let's see let's see

11 Dynamic content

이전까지는 단순 메시지를 올려 왔지만, 이젠 실제로 tutorial이 올라오게 합니다. views.py, tutorial.html을 손보아 새롭게 만들어 줍니다.

```
tutorials = [t.tutorial_slug for t in Tutorial.objects.all()]
if single_slug in tutorials:
    this_tutorial = Tutorial.objects.get(tutorial_slug =
single_slug)
    return render(request,
                  "main/tutorial.html",
                  {"tutorial": this_tutorial})

<div class="col s12, m8, l8">
        <h3>{{tutorial.tutorial_title}}</h3>
        <p style="font-size:70%">Published
{{tutorial.tutorial_published}}</p>
        {{tutorial.tutorial_content¦safe}}
</div>
```

여태는 시리즈물을 클릭했을 때 처음 올린 tutorial을 part one이라 해서 먼저 보여 준다 했습니다. 이번엔 오른편에 사이드바를 올려서 시리즈물 특정 편을 선택 url을 클릭해 바로 가 볼 수 있게 해 주고자 합니다. 여기서 우리 또 한번의 foreign key 매칭 알고리즘을 활용합니다. 지금까지 우리 모두 세 번의 매칭 알고리즘을 실습해 보았습니다.

```
tutorials = [t.tutorial_slug for t in Tutorial.objects.all()]
if single_slug in tutorials:
        this_tutorial = Tutorial.objects.get(tutorial_slug =
single_slug)
```

```
        tutorials_from_series =
Tutorial.objects.filter(tutorial_series__tutorial_series=this_tutorial.
tutorial_series).order_by("tutorial_published")
        this_tutorial_idx =
list(tutorials_from_series).index(this_tutorial)
        return render(request,
                      "main/tutorial.html",
                      {"tutorial": this_tutorial,
                       "sidebar": tutorials_from_series,
                       "this_tutorial_idx": this_tutorial_idx})
```

추가로 materializecss의 JavaScript collapsible 기능을 적용해서 커서가 놓인 곳의 시리즈물이 확대되어 튀어나와 보이게 합니다.

```
<div class="col s12, m4, l4">
    <ul class="collapsible popout">
        {% for tutorial in sidebar %}

            {% if forloop.counter0 == this_tutorial_idx %}
                <li class="active">
                    <div class="collapsible-
header">{{tutorial.tutorial_title}}<br>(currently
viewing)</div>
                </li>
            {% else %}
                <li>
                    <div class="collapsible-
header">{{tutorial.tutorial_title}}</div>
                    <div class="collapsible-body">
                        <p><a
href="/{{tutorial.tutorial_slug}}"><button class="btn waves-
effect waves-light right-align" style="background-
color:yellow; color:black">Go</button></a></p>
                    </div>
                </li>
            {% endif %}

        {% endfor %}
    </ul>
</div>
```

This tutorial now what we want to say is man my back is itching this tutorial and then i'm just trying to make it big as possible this will be a long one it's gonna run off the screen no matter what size we do so What we're gonna say is tutorials from series probably could come up with a better name But we'll stick with that we're going to say tutorial dot objects dot filter So we're going to filter by tutorial so first we need to get the tutorial series so tutorial underscore series now what's tutorial series? That tutorial series is a foreign key so we already should know that okay we're going to point to tutorial series No if we want to reference anything else under here what we're gonna need to use is the double underscore So what we will do tutorial series boom What we're trying to reference here is we want to reference the specifically the tutorial underscore series where that tutorial series is equal to this tutorial So again this is a Tutorial object Well it has an attribute tutorial series hot diggity Let's so then we're just gonna say this tutorial dot tutorial series So take a note the filter bits where we're using like attributes is a double underscore but then we're like to get it to do the equals here is we're back to python land regular land i'd love to know in the backend heymen! I'd love to know in the backend how that double underscore even works like are they using some sort of regular expressions or is this an aspect of Python I've never heard of i'd really like to know I might have to go in the backend and like see how they handled the that like what exactly are they doing there Because yeah you'd want to use dot you know but no! that doesn't work So alright so filter by a tutorial series

(12) Deployment

deploying Django to a server 해내는 마지막 단원입니다. VPS(Virtual Private Server) 가상사설 서브 서비스를 제공하는 web cloud service 사를 하나 선택하는 것이 중요하겠죠? Linode.com의 리노드사가 Harrison 이랑 십년을 같이 했다하고, 기본 월 $5 정도로 시작해 가성비가 아주 좋다 합니다. 그냥 원본 비디오를 따라 지시문에 답하면 됩니다. 일단 가입해서 내 account가 생기게 되면 이제 할 일이 connect to the server 차례입니다. Networking이라 하고, puTTy라는 원격접속 프로그램을 download 해서 이용합니다. linoid의 Networking Access에서 SSH Access IP address를 찾아내어 puTTy에 연결해 줍니다. 그래서 나오는 초기 UNIX shell 에서 Python 3를 시스템에다 깔아 줍니다. 이어서 Django도 깔아 줍니다. 이 모든 작업은 text-based tutorial에 올란 아래의 순서를 밟아서 원본 비디오랑 같이 하나씩 확인해 나가심 됩니다:

What we will need is pip for python 3:

apt-get install -y python3-pip

Then let's update pip:

python3 -m pip install --upgrade pip

Now we can install django and the tinymce app that we used so far:

python3 -m pip install django django-tinymce4-lite

Now let's make our web dir:

mkdir /var/www

Then change directory into that:

cd /var/www

Now, let's make a quick demo django project to see how things work:

django-admin startproject mysite

Change directory into that project:

cd mysite

Next, we're going to edit the settings.py file, using the editor called nano.

nano mysite/settings.py

The biggest thing is to turn off DEBUG, setting this to False.

다음 작업은 it_works라는 app을 하나 깔아 주는 일입니다. mysite/urls.py 에 있는 내용을 copy-paste 해서 새롭게 it_works 라는 이름의 app을 깔아 줍니다. 이제 우리의 app 이름은 main에서 it_works로 바뀝니다. 이렇게 해서 Django stuff 일을 모두 끝냅니다.

자, 우린 server in the cloud와 all the Django stuffs의 setup을 마쳤습니다. 이제 남은 것이 let the web server talk to django 하게 해 주는 intermediary를 필요로 합니다. WSGI Web Server Gate Interface라 합니다.

apt-get install -y apache2 libapache2-mod-wsgi-py3

여기서 apache2는 우리의 web server, and then wsgi.

다음, fill in virtual host information을 이렇게 해 줍니다.

nano /etc/apache2/sites-available/mysite.conf

이제 남은 일은 마지막 한 가지- systemct1 reload apache2 아파치를 이렇게 새로 올려 주면 됩니다.

So the next thing that we're gonna do is start a new app So we're going to python3 mysite slash manage dot py startapp and then we're gonna call this it_works cool Now we're gonna do is i think i'm gonna start copying and pasting again So let me come over here i don't want to have to like write all this stuff out This is just for like a really quick example anyway So let me scroll down to where we are it works ok So first let's CD into mysite and then we're going to nano mysite urls dot py because we have to point that to our new app so i'm going to take this copy If you hold ctrl + k and nano it deletes lines at a time so delete it all the lines paste in the code ctrl x yes enter done Now we're going to come over to the urls for the app and again that's blank so we're just gonna copy and paste that in x yes or ctrl x yes You're writing what happened? hold on! mysite Is oh oh it almost looks like we didn't get i wonder if i can't do this sort of pathing i think this is what screwed us up Let me go back one yeah ooh that's gross so let me RM-r remove recursively it works / hopefully i didn't screw us up any further Anyway yes CD mysite / ls for listed out manage dot py Let's create that one more time python3 manage.py startapp it_works ok anyway let's try that one more time nano it_works/urls.py and then copy paste that stuff in yes by the way for sure by now our stack script is done just take a note anyway now let's do the views So nana okay so take this paste those in ctrl x yes save okay cool All right that's all the Django stuff

코딩영어

나랏말씀이 미국과 달라 문자끼리 서로 맞지 아니하다 이런 까닭으로 어리석은 백성이 컴과 소통하는 랭귀지를 배우고자 할 바가 있어도 마침내 자신의 뜻을 펴지 못하는 사람이 많으니라. 내 이를 위하여 가엾게 여겨 새로 코딩학습법을 만드노니 모든 사람으로 하여금 쉽게 익혀 날마다 쓰기에 편안케 하고자 할 따름이니라.